THE STRUGGLE OF JACOB

The Struggle of Jacob

by
M. D. Molinié

translated by
Lorna Wishaw

PAULIST PRESS
New York/Ramsey/Toronto

A Deus Book edition of Paulist Press originally published under the title: *Le Combat de Jacob*© Les Editions du Cerf, 1967.

Cover Design: Morris Berman

Library of Congress
Catalog Card Number: 77-78216

ISBN: 0-8091-2036-4

Published by Paulist Press
Editorial Office: 1865 Broadway, New York, N.Y. 10023
Business Office: 545 Island Road, Ramsey, N.J. 07446

Printed and bound in the
United States of America

Contents

Contents

Introduction

We do not know how to love God because we
don't know that God loves us. We don't know he loves
us because we don't love him. And that, in sum, is the
vicious circle from which revelation tries to snatch us.

So many obscurities surround human life. Whatever certainty we have of being loved by God does not
dispel these obscurities; in fact, we must admit that at
times it augments and aggravates them. We do have
this excuse for our lack of intelligence and our weak
faith. God, who knows our misery, uses infinite patience in educating us—he brings us to love him as we
come to understand that he loves us.

This education in love has been offered secretly to
every person born into this world. And on the last day,
we shall know how this was done and whether it was
received or rejected back in the mists of time by peoples
who were strangers to Israel's history. Since Abraham,
however, we know that God's love has spoken officially; "wisdom has cried aloud at street corners," and we
are able to take possession of the Word and benefit by
its teaching.

This book is an attempt to point out the essentials
of this message as it has been received by the Church,
omitting the secondary aspects that might lessen the
impact. For the message is a cry as well as a murmur;
the cry must penetrate into our very being if we are to
be delivered from that vicious circle in which mankind

1

has been caught since the beginning.

There is no real conflict—but rather perfect continuity—between the Old Covenant and the New. The Old Covenant is an overwhelming declaration of love for which trinitarian revelation furnishes the supreme completion.[1] "God who at sundry times and diverse manners spoke in times past to the fathers by the prophets last of all in these days has spoken to us by his Son, whom he appointed heir of all things, by whom also he made the world" (Heb. 1:1-2).

The education given the sons of Abraham had the sole purpose of plunging them into adoration, and adoration is indispensable to anyone wishing to encounter Jesus Christ. It is necessary to be a Jew—that is, an adorer, a worshiper—before one can become a Christian—a friend and son. It was hard to initiate the best of Jews into this secret, and it is even more difficult for us to learn it today. God was forced to prune and pummel the hearts of his adorers, polishing them to a high luster, down through a long and animated history in order that they could attain the high, subtle level of spirituality he required to prepare the way for his Son and for the unveiling of trinitarian life.

The extraordinary education given the Jewish people is much more important to us than their ethnic peculiarities. We need this same education, and we have to obtain it by following the same route if we wish to penetrate into the mystery of Christ. The history of the Jewish people remains the one and only model for initiation into the love of God.

It is necessary then to look into the depths of adoration in our own hearts—this is the only way to keep from stamping around too loudly outside the gates of heaven. The importance of balance here is confirmed by the attention given the Psalms in the prayer of the Church. It is striking to note the use made by Christian contemplatives of the Psalms in learning both the distance separating us from God and the love that brings us so close to him. Apprenticeship with the Psalms reveals the very deep and delicate truths in which we must immerse ourselves to gain access to the still more profound and more delicate truths of trinitarian friendship.

The most tormenting and burdensome questions have not changed for us since the story of Job, or even that of Adam and Eve; the only respite for us lies in adoration. Beyond adoration, in a world inaccessible to the heart of man, lies splendor, and suffering, too, at a banquet to which Jesus Christ is inviting us. This is the splendor we shall discuss. Beyond adoration, there are no problems, and certainly no blasphemy. No exploration of the depths of spiritual life can go this far, of course, unless God himself guides us into the vast chasms of trinitarian friendship.

It is necessary for us to be initiated into the Old Covenant because we have to be supple enough to offer ourselves to the New. "And I, if I be lifted up from the earth, will draw all things to myself," Jesus said (Jn. 12:32). Jesus intends to carry us off to heaven; yet before we penetrate into new light and new darkness, we must first be initiated by Jesus and by the Church into adoration of the one true God.

The peace of Christ is an unexpected enlargement of the peace hoped for by the Jews but it is the same peace. The Incarnate Word says more to us than he did to Job, but he really only says it to those who have agreed to listen first of all to what he said to Job and throughout the Old Covenant.

The first chapter of this book will be an inquiry into the whole Bible, Old and New Testaments, so that we can glean some understanding of God's love for us and especially the way this love is expressed: how madly, unimaginably, and, finally, how crushingly he loves us!

In the second chapter we will see that in spite of appearances, we don't love God, and consequently we can't love one another or love life or anything else with any fidelity. We are condemned to remain disgusted with ourselves until we can find the Savior.

And in the final chapter, we will try to understand that we actually can achieve a love for God: "Things that are impossible with men are possible with God" (Lk. 18:27). He manages to get us to love him when we come to understand his love. Through our love for him, we are plunged ever further into the burning darkness from whose depths we are to emerge forever more into the light.

NOTE

1. Obviously the mystery of the Incarnation was absolutely new, but the novelty itself is the consummation and the crowning of a series of divine interventions. God so loved the world that in the end he gave it his only Son.

1

We Are Precious to God

Abraham's great family was quick to learn that God is transcendent. Quickly, too, they learned of the importance of man and of his works in the eyes of God. Other people, who did not have this kind of education, tended to bring God down to earth or to substitute a family of personalities, more or less roughly hewn. This is called polytheism; the Greek religion is the best known example. It is quite common to stress the refining of the Jewish concept of God and of the jealousy with which God maintained its purity. The liturgy of the Holy of Holies is a repeated and savage condemnation of idolatry and of all forms of contamination of Judaic worship by foreign cults. This is the everlasting theme of the prophets and of the "historical" books of the Bible.

Much less stress is generally laid on the extraordinary importance seemingly given by God to man throughout that history, even though this is manifested so strikingly in God's *choice* of Israel. To be sure, God is a jealous God though he is merciful, and all this because he has loved Israel with a very special love. The delightful tale of Jonah and his castor plant shows that Nineveh, and therefore all the peoples of the earth, are precious in his eyes. Here indeed is a very profound, very secret element of doctrine that is indispensable

5

both to the spirit of true adoration and to the sense of God's transcendence. The Hindu religion has risen to a notion of God that is as pure and transcendent as that of Abraham, and even more so according to some scholars. What Hinduism lacks for the formation of true worshipers[1] is not so much the sense of God as the feeling for man—his consistency, his worth, integrity, value. Consequently, there is no sense of adoration as a *dialogue* with the Creator, a dialogue that is so infinitely precious in the eyes of the Creator himself.

Lost in the Universe

The importance of man is a far more strange and disconcerting fact than the transcendence of God. It is more remote from the spontaneous conceptions of human intelligence, both for ordinary people and for philosophers. Both of these hold to a certain basic fatalism in which our destiny seems to be tossed about by forces which are beyond our comprehension and tend to crush us. It is obviously Judaeo-Christian civilization that revealed to the West the value of human life and the importance of individual initiative. The modern world's belief in action and philosophy's great interest in the "subject" spring from Christianity and its Judaic root.

I would be the first to deplore the loss of the sense of contemplation in the Christian West, but that does not mean I cultivate any nostalgia for the Eastern religions. To them, the pathetic importance that the religion of Abraham accords to human liberty and the violence of divine reaction to betrayals by the chosen people seem to reveal an inferior degree of spiritual development. No matter what the Christian philosophers have to say about the way of perfection, negative theology or the "cloud of unknowing," nothing will be taken seriously by Eastern thinkers as long as they see us giving so much importance to man's consistency and the importance of his decisions.

This, however, is precisely what makes for the superiority of Christianity and Judaism in regard to adoration. Outside the family of Abraham (including Islam), contemplation of the universe and its Creator leaves man with no alternative but to efface himself in the awareness of his own insignificance. This is the teaching of Stoicism and, despite appearances, of Epicureanism. Even Aristotle's humanism notes with a certain nostalgia that human happiness is precarious, and only with the greatest difficulty does it attain a few crumbs of divine bliss.

To the degree that the Western world is becoming paganized we can see it sliding inevitably back into this same fatalism. Men of action are becoming more resigned to a tragic view of life, tragic in the ancient sense where man struggles knowing that the world is destined to be conquered by death.[2] Modern contemplatives— that is to say, scientists—happily rally around a concept of evolution at whose end everything must relapse or else explode in a big bang, a sort of "stupefying radio-diffusion" (cf. James Jeans).[3]

Skepticism, the Root of Infidelity

If the adoration taught to the Jews outdistances all other forms of worship, it is precisely because there is a point of convergence when divine transcendence and

human consistency, instead of competing, merge to re-
inforce one another. God's transcendency gives man his
consistency. It is very difficult for us to appreciate this;
we are constantly tempted to set the Creator into com-
petition with his creature because the secret of God
eludes us and our consistency depends on this secret.
The most perfect homage we can give to the all-powerful God is to affirm our consistency before his face.

Thus, there is no sense in doing things by halves,
no use in parsimoniously measuring out the quantity of
importance accorded to man. Rather, we must stress simultaneously God's transcendence and man's importance—not despite one another but because of one another. Furthermore, at the very moment in adoration
where man discovers his own nothingness before his
Creator, he discovers by his very existence that his adoration is of value, and, consequently, that he is the creature, the adorer. This, of course, is an odd sort of paradox, for if, indeed, God alone is important, why should
it be important for man to recognize this fact? The answer is that man is precious in God's eyes because he
adores.

The tradition of Israel is profoundly aware of this
paradox. Her prophets knew the temptations that lurk,
waiting to empty adoration of all substance; they were
especially alive to the danger of the fatalism of which
we are speaking. "What is man that you should be
mindful of him, or the son of man that you should care
for him?" (Ps. 8:5 and Job 7:17-18). This was the fundamental skepticism that everlastingly threatened the
Jewish people, the secret root perhaps of all her infideli-
ties. "Say not: I am hidden from God; in heaven who
remembers me? Among so many people I cannot be
known; what am I in the world of spirits?" (Sir. 16:14-
15).

The adoration God demanded of Israel was not in fact merely natural; it was founded on the revelation of his love. We shall talk about that love now.

A Very Special Love

It is hard to imagine what religion would be like in a world where grace did not intervene. Certainly, the adoration of which we are speaking could not be nourished by awareness of God's special love for man. Nor could life be lived as a response pure and simple (and how infinitely poor) to this love—even if the temptation to regard God as hostile and indifferent could be set aside and our response were permeated by a sense of divine goodness. The best that could be said is that God would seem, in the words of C. S. Lewis, like:

> a grandfather in heaven, a senile benevolence who, as they say, "liked to see young people enjoying themselves," and whose plan for the universe was simply that it might be truly said at the end of each day that "a good time was had by all."[6]

Lewis goes on to say:

> I might, indeed, have learned even from the poets that love is something more stern and splendid than mere kindness: that even the love between the sexes is, as in Dante, "a lord of terrible aspect." There is kindness in love: but love and kindness are not coterminous, and when kindness (in the sense given above) is separated from the other elements of love, it involves a certain fundamental indiffer-

ence to its object, and even something like contempt of it. Kindness consents very readily to the
removal of its object—we have all met people
whose kindness to animals is constantly leading
them to kill animals lest they should suffer.
Kindness, merely as such, cares not whether its object becomes good or bad, provided only that it escapes suffering. As scripture points out, it is bas-
tards who are spoiled; the legitimate sons who are
to carry on the family tradition are punished (Heb.
12:8). It is for people whom we care nothing about
that we demand happiness on any terms: with our
friends, our lovers, our children, we are exacting
and would rather see them suffer much than be
happy in contemptible and alienated ways. If God
is love, he is, by definition, something more than
mere kindness. And it appears, from all records,
that though he has often rebuked us and condemned us, he has never regarded us with contempt. He has paid us the intolerable compliment
of loving us, in the deepest, most tragic, most inexorable sense.

The Choice of a People

Thus we are able to glimpse something of the wisdom that governed the election of a people, a choice
that appears to have excluded all others until the proc-
lamation by St. Paul that the Gentiles were invited to
the same banquet. As a matter of fact, Israel would
have been incapable of understanding that God loves us
if this love had not been presented as a preferential love
quite different from anything we could think up on

behalf of our God or gods. The Jewish people (and through them the whole human race) had first to be initiated into the fact—so very hard to assimilate—that an *extraordinary love* weighed upon them. And this initiation actually required a contrast between this extraordinary love and the benevolence of providence in regard to the rest of the world.[8]

Incredible Promises

The abiding sense of God's teaching to Israel led her to understand that she was loved not "like all the rest" but with a special love as though she were a bride, which is probably the best image. Between the first words spoken to Abraham and the Song of Songs, there runs a perfect continuity; the Old Testament is incomprehensible if this continuity is broken. To be sure, the ultimate secrets of this love were yet to be unveiled, both in depth (the mystery of the Holy Trinity) and in extension (the call to the Gentiles). The essential had been given, however. It lay in the idea of Israel's special election, and it prevented her from attributing to God a more or less vague platonic love, which is the only kind of love we would be able to imagine without revelation.

It is then easy to understand the continual temptation facing the Jews; it is the same temptation that faces us today. Over and over, it has been called idolatry. It seems to me, however, that the root of the danger goes far deeper, and that it lies waiting for us with an ever-increasing and unsuspected vigor. It is a question, in a word, of doubt—doubt not of the existence of God nor of his basic goodness but of the *extraordinary* nature of his love for us. This doubt was familiar to the mass of Jewish people and massively indeed they succumbed to it, turning to the Baals and the Astartes. And yet though all the prophets came face to face with this doubt and were torn and tormented by it, they never succumbed.

Abraham might have become a skeptic at the very start, for divine promises were never fulfilled very quickly. Those promises had their little twist of humor for Abraham and Sarah to laugh at rather than cry about—to the disgust of the visitor from Mambré. After the miracle of Isaac's birth came the miracle of the sacrifice. Isaac's birth was an example of the state of affairs that exists between God and his servants; they are forever faced with contradictions that no amount of wisdom can explain away or overcome. Here, on the one hand, the repeated assertion of God's extraordinary and jealous love, supported externally by extraordinary signs and internationally by an all-consuming "hope against hope." Yet, on the other hand, the facts: innumerable, unarguable, substantial! And then there is human nature with all its complexity, which left to itself, tumbles unresisting into doubt (seemingly so well justified) that things just couldn't be as they appear, that it is all a dream, a fairy tale. This is the point where Satan lies waiting to drag his victim beyond doubt into the dizzy vortex of nothingness, into the shadows of anguish where God is not.

He Has Done Everything To Shatter My Faith in Him

We saw the ghastly, apocalyptic level this "everything" can attain in the last World War. More than ever, perhaps, Israel's vocation manifested its terrifying character, as though God was seeking at any price to bring her fate into line with that of his Son. "I am proud to be a Jew because it is so hard, so very hard to be one. I am glad to belong to the most unhappy race on earth, for whom the Torah is the supreme moral code and the most splendid of laws." These are the words of a Jew going to his death during the revolt of the Warsaw ghetto in 1943:

Something very surprising is going on in the world. It is the time that the All-Powerful has turned his face from his suppliants. God has hidden his face from the world. So this is why men have been abandoned to their most savage passions. It is natural when such passions are let loose in the world, that the first victims should be those in whom the pure and the divine is still alive.

This is by no means comforting; yet the fate of our people is settled by the laws of heaven and not by earthly laws. Anyone who sees these happenings through the eyes of faith is bound to see them as part of a divine settling of accounts, in the face of which human tragedies have no significance. This doesn't mean that the pious Jew simply accepts the judgment as it comes, saying: "God is right, his judgment is just." To say simply that we deserve the blows we receive would only show that we despise ourselves and that we hold in contempt the name of God.

Because things are as they are, naturally I don't expect any miracles, and neither do I pray to God to have mercy on me. Let him show me the same indifference he has shown to so many millions: I am not an exception to the rule, and I don't expect him to accord me any special attention. I'm not going to try to save myself and I shan't try to escape from here. Rather, I shall help the work by soaking my clothes with gasoline (I have three bottles left of the dozens I have poured onto the heads of the criminals). These bottle are as dear to me as wine that inebriates. As soon as I have poured the last drop over myself, I shall put this letter into the empty bottle and then I shall hide it among the half-cemented stones around the window. Later, should anyone find it, he will be able to know a little about the feelings of a Jew, one of the millions who are dead, a Jew abandoned by the God in whom he believed so intensely.

I believe in the God of Israel, even though he has done everything to shatter my faith in him. No longer is my relationship with him one of the servant to his master, but rather of a disciple toward his master. I believe in his laws, even though I may challenge the justice of his actions. I bow down before his greatness, but I will not kiss the rod that beats me. I love him but I love his law even more. Even had I been wrong about him, I would continue to worship his law. The meaning of God is religion, but his law means the wisdom of life. You say that we have sinned. Obviously we have sinned. I am ready to admit that we should be punished for that. All the same I'd like you to tell me whether there is a sin in all the world that deserves this kind of punishment. I am saying all this to you, my God, because I believe in you, because I believe in you more than ever, because now I know that you are my God and not the God of those whose actions are the vile fruit of their militant impiety.

I cannot praise you for the deeds you tolerate, but I bless you and praise you for your awe-inspiring majesty. Indeed your majesty must be very great since you are unimpressed by all that is going on now.

Death cannot hurt me now. I must stop writing. From the floors above, the shooting is growing weaker every minute. The last defenders of our hideout have just fallen, and with them has fallen our great and beautiful Jewish Warsaw that feared God. The sun is setting, and I thank God that I shall never see it rise again. Crimson rays are slanting through the window, and the flaming patch of sky that I can see from here is flowing like molten gold. In an hour at the very most, I shall join my wife and children and the millions of the children of my people in a better world untroubled by doubt, where the one sovereign is God.

I die in peace but unsatisfied; a man overcome but not despairing; a believer but not a suppliant; a lover of God but not a blind man mouthing Amen. I have followed God even when he has driven me far from him. I have kept his commandments even as he struck me in payment for my obedience. I have loved him. I was in love with him, and I still am, even though he has humbled me to the earth, even though he has tortured me unto death, even though he has reduced me to derision and shame.

You may torture me to my very death, but I shall still believe in you. In spite of you, I shall love you forever. And here are my last words, O my God of wrath. You will not succeed (in making me disown you). You have done everything to make me doubt you. But I shall die as I have lived, my faith in you unshaken.

Throughout eternity, be thou praised, thou God of the dead, God of vengeance, God of truth and faith. Thou wilt turn thy countenance toward the world once more and shake its foundations with your all-powerful voice.

Hear, O Israel: Eternal is our God; Eternal is the One and Only.[10]

The Mystery of Job

And so the mystery of Job goes on until the end of time. The most cruel aspect, perhaps, of Job's predicament was that God never relaxed his pressure, even in the darkest times. Without that, there would have been no problem. Of course, there would have been suffering, but not that suffering, not that unique kind of darkness. Job had known that he was loved by God; he had had time to be blinded, stupefied, inebriated by the tenderness of God.[11] Later, there still remained something within him that stopped him from no longer believing. This kind of hope is precisely the most agonizing of all—confronted by divine behavior that surely cannot be love, nor, alas, even indifference, but rather a pitiless malevolence, justified by the inaccessible transcendence which Job continued to worship even as he raged against it.

We shall have to understand why adoration, and only adoration, can reach beyond all contradictions and far beyond all wisdom. It is brought about by plunging without reserve into the heart of darkness—in the absolute certainty of God's love, or in the frequent impression (at least, at the time) of God's non-love, yet plunging on, accepting no diminution in intensity of adoration. In the wake of such suffering comes questioning, distressed, passionate questioning—sometimes leading to the edge of revolt (but a loving revolt) as in Job's case, sometimes pervaded by exultation in the expectancy of the eternal response as in the Psalms, but in all cases a questioning that is never silenced and that is truly shuddering for those who adore in spirit and in truth.

It is not a matter of being resigned to the inability to understand. The laziness of those who refuse to rack their brains is destined to be routed and crushed just as is the greed of those who demand understanding at any cost. No one is exempt from this argument with God, because God desires this argument (and herein lies the mystery of Job). Simple souls do not need grand theology to be upset by the mystery of evil or to accuse God with the passion and anger that is born of love—anger that is greatly preferred by God to the tepid, soothing arguments of Job's friends who, after all, were not themselves in much hurry to take the trip toward the vision. Of course, Job needed to be put in his place, but, after all, that is what he had been asking for. He yearned to be overwhelmed by the light, to be shown his own stupidity. Because Job *loved* God, he wanted to be stripped of his impurity by the divine response.

The Game of Love and Chance

Without revelation, mankind is immersed in a darkness beyond the reach of delivering wisdom. When the Word of God throws light into that darkness, the darkness is not dispelled as might be hoped. Rather, it is intensified, for the obscurity deepens as the light progresses. And so it goes, until man meets his God face to face.

It is strange indeed to know that you are a being distinct from the Creator. But it is infinitely stranger to know that you are loved with a unique love, an unimaginable, consuming love. That should solve all problems, or better still scatter them; instead it multiplies them, leaving us in a state where everything seems to be settled by chance. This impression is unavoidable since chance does seem to play a real hand in the world. And what an obvious hand it plays—enormous, stupid, even at times monstrous! All, then, is ruled by love and all is ruled by chance. At this point, understanding gives up, and wisdom cannot help for there is no wisdom that can include at one time that special kind of love and the stupidity of evil.

"This Is No Longer True for Me"

Job's friends proposed, on the other hand, a pernicious kind of adoration opting away from Jewish revelation, a more or less hidden descent into pagan fatalism, a diminishing of the sheer courage of faith. It is normal, as I've said, that a certain amount of doubt prowls about in our souls all the time and that Satan will nourish this doubt. It is even normal for one to give in to this doubt for varied lengths of time (only a few saints have resisted this perfectly). But it is scandalous to justify this falling-away by attributing it to the so-called demands made upon us by adoration.

A faltering in faith can, of course, be caused by clumsy or superficial reading matter, or by poorly guided or premature reading of the great traditional works on providence or divine government. Here, for instance, is a rather upsetting testimony of a Carmelite nun, aged 66 years:

Father B., who was my spiritual director, encouraged me to read the *Treatise on God*. I got as far as the chapter on predestination and the small number of the elect. It took me a long time to recover from the staggering blow I received. It was not so much that I was worried about my own salvation, but up until then, I had thought of the loss of souls as due to their own somewhat perverted wills; I was about to say, as though God himself could do nothing to help them. The focus given by Saint Thomas was so terrible to me because it was a source of temptation to believe no longer in love in the same way as I had. I have never regretted having been brought in this way to a more just notion of God's transcendence, of his inaccessible mystery. I pulled out of it by adoration but perhaps I lost the naive, childlike boldness that thinks all things are permitted. Now I am scarcely able to ask God for anything, for myself or for others, except for that which he wants to give me. Perhaps this attitude is more real, but the spontaneity is gone. And I must admit that thinking back on phrases in the Gospel such as "Ask and you shall receive that your joy may be perfect," I am tempted to say: "This is no longer true for me." As I grow older, everything that might have lighted my way has gone out, and I am now living my contemplative life, or what should be one, in total darkness, with long periods that are very painful. I have absolutely no sense of the presence of God or of the reality of divine life with us that demands a positive act of faith, so that I am most often left with the mystery of evil that invades everything and seems to submerge all the rest. This is my usual state of suffering, and there is nothing to counterbalance it.[12]

This seems to be similar to Job's situation, for the mystery of such suffering did not disappear with Christ. The light of the Gospels, far from suppressing the darkness surrounding Job, can instead make it more profound and more agonizing. The nun sees the decreasing boldness of her conviction of being loved as a temptation. One hopes that she is able to resist it and that in the burning darkness the Holy Spirit is purifying her confidence.

It is disturbing, however, that she should see her temptation as something in opposition to more pure adoration. Such excessive resignation is but the backwash of a grief born of doubt, against which she continues to struggle.

Painfully or Joyfully According to the Weather

Job's adoration was, on the other hand, characterized by an absence of such resignation. He shouts at God, expecting a reply but well aware that God is not obliged to make one. Yet the fire within his bones keeps him from knuckling under, and he protests his innocence to his Redeemer with scandalous violence, very close to blasphemy. Yet this is the road leading to the purest adoration, the most perfect worship, the kind that believes no matter what may happen, with a mad, ever increasing faith in God's love—not in spite of God's transcendence but because of it, and because he draws from this transcendence a blind, ecstatic confidence that is in the end the purest form of worship. There is no anesthetized, lethargic acceptance of the darkness, but a recognition of God's free gift of love and a burning belief in it despite all appearances to the contrary—a belief that is anxious, questioning, vivid, somersaulting, and, humanly speaking, most imperfect. This is the only way to peace that God has given us.

The supreme achievement of Jewish revelation is to give man the maximum of his own consistency, importance and value. Even as man stands before his God of love, he acknowledges painfully or joyfully, according to the weather, that he is no more than a wisp of straw in the hand of God, a "speck of dust lost in infinity."

Adoration unfolds continuously, under the implacable light of God's love, a love that is far more crushing than his transcendence alone. The terrible, concrete awareness of this love is the wellspring of the deepest joy, deeper far than all human joy. And yet, as long as we have not been purified, it is also the source of anguished suffering and distress in some ways more acute than the sense of having been abandoned by God in a sort of indifference.[14] There are times indeed when in our lassitude and impurity we would willingly have recourse to his indifference, if only to escape from the blazing vigilance which numbers every hair of our heads. For we, like Job, find this as intolerable as the fury of the mid-day sun.[15]

It is then, of course, that we tend to slide into fatalism, or at least to a perspective that accords us less value in God's eyes and less importance to our actions, so that we risk downgrading our adoration all the more, and not least by not recognizing or by diminishing God's transcendence. Or, to explain it another way, the first blow we strike is our refusal to recognize the infinite value we have in God's eyes. Next and as a result of this, we downgrade our idea of God until it becomes no more than a reflection of our own image and likeness. Both are attacks against pure adoration, but the first failure is far more dangerous and difficult to avoid than the second. The latter can be avoided when there has been sound formation, though the obscurity surrounding man's consistency in God's eyes must be acknowledged. Faith, however, gives a new dimension to this consistency, making it almost divine in scope even though more obscure than ever. Now we must plunge into the heart of night with the courage of young Saint Thérèse of Lisieux or of Job. Both were the same—refusing to give an inch of ground even to the most subtle temptations that risk corrupting adoration.

Trinitarian Revelation

To repeat and conclude, the Old Covenant was a perfect teaching, aimed at disengaging pious Jews from a too human, too vaguely fatalistic idea of divine transcendence. It made them aware of the almost incomprehensible predilection weighing upon them, a predilection so very extraordinary that when Israel was unfaithful, God played the amazing role not of a person who abandons his friends in anger but of one who complains in pain and grief and rage at having been abandoned.

What Israel was unable to understand, however, was that God's predilection would concern all of mankind. Had Israel realized this, the love of God would probably have been dissipated into a vague, universal motion of divine benevolence. Before God revealed his very special love for all mankind, he first demonstrated what was so precious and unexpected about this love.

This revelation was the task of the Trinity. Following two thousand years of preparation, the Holy Trinity was offered to the Jews and to all humanity. Without that two thousand years of preparation, the Trinity could not have been intelligible: "Listen, O Israel! I have loved you with an eternal love. . . . And why have I loved you? Not because you are lovable, for you are the poorest of people, and you were not lovable before you were loved. It is my love that made you lovable and gave you life. Why then have I loved you? Because I am love." All through history, this is what the prophets revealed to the Jewish people.

The revelation of the Trinity has nothing different to say; it just goes much further in the same direction. It spreads out before us like the edge of a lava flow. We must study this flow to understand that it leads us to the heart of God.

God Begot a Son and Their Love Was Given to Us

It is not necessary to study theology to understand these two truths, to take them seriously and to appreciate their weight. God is not the Father in a vague sort of way as an artist is father of his work. Works of art are born from thought and feeling, not from blood and guts. And even if it were possible (the torment of every genius) to realize Pygmalion's dream of giving life and speech to his statue, she would still not be his child in the visceral sense. Fashioned by his hands and by his dreams, she would be what he wanted her to be but she would not be made by that obscure biological process to which man abandons himself and over which he has no control. Here lies the crucifying aspect of human paternity: man's great desire to make children "after his own image and likeness" is doomed to failure, sometimes to the most drastic failure. Nevertheless, this secret mystery of flesh drawn from uncharted depths gives an irreplaceable zest to the act of generation: "bone of my bone and flesh of my flesh" as Genesis reports. That such a mystery exists in God, Jesus Christ has taught us and only Jesus. In God the mystery exists with a splendor, a light and a fidelity that are unknown on human generation. The Father was not deceived in

his Son; between them there was not the slightest dissonance. With the delicacy of spiritual fruit, the "candor
of the eternal light" poured from the depths of God
with a virtually biological power that in man is the
most blind, the most ravaging of forces.

Christians mechanically reciting the Lord's Prayer
have used trinitarian words ever since. They are the
world's echo of the Son's reply to his Father's "This
day I have eternally begotten you." In a more general
way, any impulse toward God is trinitarian. The tears
of Mary Magdalene at the feet of Jesus, the light that
struck at the heart of the good thief as he looked at
Jesus on the cross, the enthusiasm of Zechariah—these
were real happenings. No psychologist can explain what
these events were, what really took place. They were
caused by a spring whose source was invisible to man, a
groundswell set off by the Trinity, rolling in to die at
the edge of the human heart. The events of the Gospels
being elementary, at times tough feelings come into
play—the crowd rushing in to be fed, or some sudden
tears, or an action as simple as the breaking of a jar of
perfume. "How awesome is this place! This is none
other but the house of God; this is the gate of heaven"
(Gen. 28:17).

We Are the Gift of God

Ever since Jesus Christ spoke to us, we men and
women, in searching to know what we are and to understand the things that happen to us, have had to look
into the infinite love that flows between the Father and
the Son in the Trinity. Saint Paul and all Christian
tradition agree that we are adopted sons. Yet there is

much more here than adoption in the usual sense of the
word. Human adoption does not involve the power to
make those chosen into perfect copies of sons born into
the family. "And because you are sons, God has sent
the Spirit of his Son into our hearts, crying "Abba! Father' " (Gal. 4:6). All of trinitarian revelation is
required to lead us to the profound meaning of this
divine paternity for us. The Holy Spirit did not make
us mere honorary sons kept at a distance by the unbrid-
geable chasm that separates the created from the uncreated, human nature from the divine. It traced in
each of us the face of the only Son—not other faces
more or less resembling the model, but that very face
that came forth from the Father and is reflected by a
multitude of the elect, with thousands of variations, so
that Jesus is indeed the "first-born of a multitude of
brothers" (Rom. 8:29).

At this level, whether we speak of God or of ourselves, *it is the same thing*. So great is the gift of God
that we hardly dare to measure its depths: we are the
gift of God—that is our supreme definition, the new
name inscribed on the white stone of the Apocalypse.
Trinitarian revelation would make no sense for us if it
were not at the same time a revelation of what we are
ourselves: ineffable, inscrutable as God, according to
the name no one knows but he to whom it is given.

Having lifted the veil from these last depths of his
love, God was able to say to the Jews: "You now know
the depth of my love, so I shall lift the veil and show
you the planetary breadth of this love, which until now
I had held secret.[17] For now that the Holy Spirit has
taught you, putting into your hearts all that I have said
to you (cf. Jn. 14:26), you are able to understand that
this love concerns all mankind without ceasing to be a

love of predilection, the kind of love in fact that is given only to *one* person, someone unique, someone necessary. For you are not my sons in name only, but truly my unique Son, so that if you should abandon me, I shall lose my Son."

NOTES

1. No matter what may be the religious life of Hindus, we are considering only doctrine here.

2. This philosophy is perceptible in all spy and crime literature.

3. Of course, there will always be optimists who dream of mutations and supermen. But these dreams are condemned to death by their very substance. They have lost the meaning of the true importance of man that, strictly speaking, can only be seen through the eyes of Jewish and Christian revelation. It matters little whether they are trying to prolong the agony, or whether they are persuading themselves that the agony is an apotheosis. At the heart of their dreams, they have accepted the idea that man is but living dust lost in the universe. This is quite enough to strip life of all significance and all value, whether they admit it or not.

"There is no God, no universe, no human race, no life on earth, no heaven, no hell. All is an absurd, grotesque dream. Nothing exists but you. And you are nothing but a thought, a lost thought, a useless thought, an orphan thought wandering solitary across everlasting nothingness" (Mark Twain, cited by Robert Escarpit in *Open Letter to God*, ed. Albin Michel, 1966, p. 129). Escarpit adds: "As for me, I love!" Such an admission is eloquent enough.

4. The other danger, of course, is the conscious pride of being a chosen people, forgetting that divine predilection is a free gift—having the illusion of deserving it all or of having nothing to fear as regards becoming unworthy. The prophets fought desperately against all this, and this aspect is the most striking of their efforts.

Such effort in itself, however, would lose significance if one were to gain the impression that "all is vanity," so well expressed in Ecclesiastes. This unedifying prophet seems to agree with the fatalism of pagan wisdom. Certainly he expresses, on the one hand, what truth is found in such wisdom, scattering the illusions which raise human agitation to fever heat. But on the other hand, he preserves Israel from fatalism; with pitiless clarity he shows its consequences. The apparent absurdity of the human condition is not hidden, but the even greater absurdity of "wisdom" claiming to go beyond it, as well as all revolt against the situation, is affirmed with the same force devoted to the vanity of all things. Thus "there is nothing better for a man to eat and drink and provide himself with good things" (Eccl. 2:24).

There is nothing soothing about this book; it is intentionally irritating and anxious, for it denounces all false solutions and bars the way to the arrogant philosophies to which men are tempted to appeal, in order to suggest even baser solutions, presented in such a disillusioned tone that no one could possibly be attracted to them.

5. We know that such a situation is not repugnant to God (grace, after all, is a free gift; it is not an obligation). We do not, however, know if this is acceptable to divine wisdom. Perhaps we even have reason to suspect that it is not, insofar as the aim of the whole of creation is to receive the gift of grace.

6. C. S. Lewis, *The Problem of Pain* (London: Collins, Fontana Books, 1940, 1972), p. 28.

7. C. S. Lewis, *ibid.*, pp. 28-29.

8. Christian theologians risk compromising our hope if they put divine predilection in regard to Israel on the same plane as the predestination of the chosen. We have to face this mystery and I am not going to avoid it. But I must stress at once that it is most dangerous to suppose that it is nothing but the pure and simple fruit of *predilection*, because this has quite a different meaning. It refers to choosing Israel from among all other peoples, and in a broader sense to the choice of all those to whom God has given more and from whom he demands more. This is in no way a pre-judgment by God of their fidelity and their endurance. After all, it was Israel, the well-beloved, who rejected the Messiah, and it was Judas who

betrayed his master. And it is those whom God *really* loves above others who have the terrible power of the most profound descent into the mystery of sin: "These wounds I received in my own home . . ." and they were not inflicted by Pharaoh.

It is very crude to set on the same level the impenetrable wisdom that permits the catastrophe of sin (a far more accessible level) with the choosing of privileged persons who are to manifest the splendor of God's love. This manifestation supposes the freedom to refuse such love. And if we claim that those who refuse were *in fact* less loved we strip almost all meaning from the words in which God complains of having cultivated a vineyard and having been rejected by it.

9. These doubts come later, unless they concern an attack by the devil whose rule is to aim at the imagination rather than at the intelligence as such.

10. Jossell Rachower, "Testament dans la fournaise" *Bible et vie chretienne* 64 (July-August 1965), pp. 72-74.

11. "When I look at the years gone by, I can say—insofar as a man can testify to anything with certainty—that I have had a magnificent life. In the past, my life was blessed with happiness, but I was never presumptuous. My door was always open to all men in need and I found happiness when I was able to be of use to my neighbor. I served God with intense abandon, and my one prayer to him was that I be able to serve him with all my heart, with all my soul, and with all my strength" (*ibid.*, p. 71).

12. *Dieuleur suffit. Le témoignage des cloitrés* (Paris: Ed. du Cerf, 1962), p. 195.

13. Certainly our purification is worked in darkness, a fact that the devil constantly tries to take advantage of. But this does not mean that worship, grown less bold or self-confident, is a "more true attitude," *even as adoration*, than one that refuses the solution of being loved less in the name of a "more correct notion of God's transcendence."

14. Actually things are not quite that simple—the impression of being abandoned by God comes precisely from the obscurity that surrounds and seemingly contradicts the impression of being loved. This is infinitely painful, but it is rooted in the pressure that God weighs upon us. Anyone who has not been subjected to this pressure will be unaware of the

joy it gives, and also the suffering. There is perhaps the nostalgia of feeling that God is far away, absent, inaccessible, but it will not be the tortured nostalgia of Kafka's heroes.

15. "Let me alone, that I may recover a little before I go whence I shall not return" (Job 10:20-21).

16. "What is man, that you should make much of him or pay him any heed? You observe him with each new day and try him at every moment! How long will it be before you look away from me and let me alone long enough to swallow my spittle? Though I have sinned, what can I do to you, O watcher of men? Why have you set me up as an object of attack; or why should I be a burden to you? Why do you not pardon my offenses or take away my guilt? For soon I shall lie down in the dust; and should you seek me I shall then be gone" (Job 7:17-21).

17. "As the Father has loved me, I also have loved you. . . . No longer do I call you servants. . . . But I have called you friends, for all things that I have heard from my Father I have made known to you" (Jn. 15:9, 15).

2
The Love of God

Human language has different levels of seriousness. Sometimes we chat about the weather, while at other times we expound on some scientific theory that seems important to us. Then there is the kind of talk that is more privileged and intuitive when we try to say something intimate and precious. Yet none of these is as profound as the words we use when we offer our life and heart to another.

Because the Word of God has this profound significance (God loved us first), it is called revelation. When one has revealed his love, he has said all there is to say, even though he still remains hidden. There is no need for further talk. All has been given. Whatever disclosures may follow will be no more than a gradual taking over of that which is already possessed.

Submission or Gift-of-Self?

Yet the recipient has to *accept* the love that has been offered to him, and it is for this reason that revelation also involves a question—the most frightening of all questions, the only one God has proposed to men. Why frightening? Because one cannot accept love without giving it in return. Love can only be repaid with love. There is no pricetag attached; love is free, yet we cannot accept without repaying in kind. At this level there is no difference between giving and receiving. They are one—we receive and respond with our hearts.

Even in loving on the human level, we often deceive ourselves, thinking we can accept love without responding with an equal gift. We make use of love but do not respond, and consequently only the surface effects of love are felt. The flavor and sweetness of real love are never known, because love has been exploited, not possessed. This is why God has no need to protect his love or to be cautious about bestowing it. As long as we are unable to respond deeply—to let go and hold nothing back—love escapes us. We possess nothing.

It is not surprising, then, that men of good will become discouraged; they ask themselves if the Christian life is practical. Instead of responding to God as he requires, with a total, almost insane love, we fall into the habit of substituting veneration. We prostrate ourselves before him while at the same time holding him at arm's length. Instead of a total gift-of-self, we prefer submission. This is sad; it is the easy way out—to offer a bent back instead of a bared breast. In this posture, we try to be just, to offer what is due to God and neighbor. Yet as long as such "justice" contains none of the secret leaven of love, it is no better than that of the scribes and Pharisees. Submitting oneself in place of giving oneself is a desperate effort. A spirit that is not given in love remains centered on self, and this self-centered state is a kind of sin; indeed it is the sin, even when sincere efforts are made to "limit the damage" by recognition of the Kingdom and the rights of the all-powerful God. No matter what a man does to "put God into his life," he will always seem to be giving at once too little and too much—simply because each partner requires all, and because the endless negotiations to set things right while holding something back, no matter how small, are hopeless. C S. Lewis once observed:

> As a young man wants a regular allowance from his father which he can count on as his own, within which he makes his own plans (and rightly, for his father is, after all, a fellow creature), so men desire to be "their own boss, to take care of their own future, to plan for pleasure and security, to have something from which, no doubt, they would pay reasonable tribute to God in the way of time, attention and love, by which is theirs, not his. They want, as we say, to "call their souls their own." But that means to live a lie, for our souls are not, in fact, our own. They want some corner in the universe of which they can say to God, "This is our business, not yours." But such does not exist.[1]

Does God Ask for Too Much?

Such truths are hard to accept, and it is difficult to admit that so total a love is really obligatory. What lies there, we tend to think, is a sublime thing, so sublime as to be quite out of the reach of the poor elementary restrictions of the human heart. When people talk of such things, we envision ourselves transported to the heart of perfection, to the mystery of charity. Grace could ask it of a saint, but it is death to human nature, and the simple moral law is much less demanding.

Many of the wise doctors of Christianity have surrendered to this illusion, and the testimony of so-called "spiritual men" has also favored it. They are aware of the terrible daily battles we must wage against our natural egoism—an egoism so deep-seated that most people think of it as a normal expression of human nature.

The truth is that nature is defiled and grace betrayed by this kind of thinking, almost to the point of blasphemy against the Author of grace and nature. C. S. Lewis here issues a severe (and at times racy) warning:

If all the boys fail an examination, surely the test must have been too hard! So all the teachers at the school feel until they learn that there are other schools where ninety percent of the boys passed the same test. Then they begin to suspect the fault did not lie with the examiners. Again, many of us have had the experience of living in some local pocket of human society—some particular school, college regiment or profession—where the environment was poor. Inside that pocket, certain actions were regarded as normal ("Everybody does it") and certain others as involving impractical or outlandish virtues. Yet when we emerged from that society, we made the horrible discovery that in the outer world, our "normal" was the kind of thing no one ever dreamed as doing, while our "outlandish" was taken for granted as the minimum standard of decency. What seemed to us to be morbid baroque scruples as long as we were in the pocket has now turned out to be the only moments of sanity we enjoyed there.

It is wise to face the possibility that the whole

human race (being a small thing in the universe) is, in fact, just such a local pocket of evil, an isolated bad school or regiment inside which minimum decency passes for heroic virtue and utter corruption for pardonable imperfection.

But is there any evidence—except Christian doctrine itself—that this is so? I am afraid there is.

In the first place, there are those odd people among us who do not accept the local standards, who demonstrate the alarming truth that a quite different behavior is, in fact, possible. Worse still, there is the fact that these people, even when widely separated in space and time, have a suspicious knack of agreeing with one another in the main— almost as if they were in touch with some larger public opinion outside the pocket. What is common to Zarathrusta, Socrates, Gotama, Christ and Marcus Aurelius is something pretty substantial.

Thirdly, we find in ourselves even now a theoretical approval of this behavior which no one practices. Even inside the picket we do not say that justice, mercy, fortitude and temperance are of *no* value, but only that the local custom is just as brave, temperate and merciful as can reasonably be expected. It begins to look as if the neglected school rules even inside this bad school were connected with some larger world—and that when the term ends we might find ourselves facing the public opinion of the larger world.

But the worst of all is this: we cannot help seeing

that only the degree of virtue that we now regard as impracticable can possibly save our race from disaster even on this planet.

The standard which seems to have come into the pocket from outside turns out to be terribly relevant to conditions inside the pocket—so relevant that a consistent practice of virtue by the human race even for ten years would fill the earth from pole to pole with peace, plenty, health, merriment and heart's ease, and nothing else will.

It may be the custom down here to treat the regimental rules as a dead letter or a counsel of perfection, but even now, everyone who stops to think can see that when we meet the enemy this neglect is going to cost every man of us his life. It is then that we shall envy the "morbid" person, the "pedant" or the "enthusiast" who really *has* taught his company to shoot and dig and spare their water bottles.[2]

Existence Demands Oblation

For us moral rectitude has become not only impractical but downright unintelligible. The innocence, sought after and found by the saints, seems to belong to another planet if not to the splendors of heaven. The Kingdom of heaven, however, is far more than that. We must pray for healing, for the grace that our eyes may be opened to the beauty of the law of love. For then and only then shall we be able to understand both the depths to which sin has led us and the heights to which God has called us.

The teaching of Saint Thomas can be a powerful help in cleaning up our intelligence. The gift-of-self seems heroic and inaccessible to our natural strength because we believe that we are fatally involved from birth in a quest for personal good, just as animals quest for well-being. The only escape from this egocentricity, we think, lies in making a great leap to surpass ourselves, either by sheer will power or by some terrifying miraculous effect of grace. Jansenism stems in part from this kind of thinking, and Jansenism has also helped it take root so solidly in the hearts of men that it is almost impossible to imagine that things could be different. To most of us, God seems to be a "stern man" who reaps where he has not sowed (Mt. 25:24), who makes a human nature that is in all innocence forever impelled to quest for its own good and then requires it to turn itself from this quest and love him above everything else. An invasion of grace would then require the denial and destruction of all that is deep and rich and sacred in the heart of man. As for expecting a purely moral law to bring about such Abrahamic sacrific, it is utterly unthinkable.

To this kind of thinking, Saint Thomas quietly opposed the famous principle which has been adopted by the Church: *divine grace does not destroy nature*. Few understand the vast meaning of this truth. To be sure, grace goes beyond human nature, as we shall see; yet it rests upon nature and is rooted in a vital impulse that is achieved and perfected by the grace that consumes it.

Of course, there are sacrifices in Christian life, but they are not caused by conflicts or tensions between *innocent* nature and grace. God does not reap where he has not sown and he does not demand what he has not given. Even before the invitation to trinitarian life, moral law invites us to love God above all things, ourselves included. The mainspring of this love was inserted within us at the moment of our creation—we all have been hurled into existence in a state of oblation. The first commandment requires us to respect this vital initial impulse to the very end; it expects us to carry out consciously on our own level that which is carried out blindly by all living creatures on their level: the ecstatic worship of the Creator.

Man in his intelligence, driven by the obscure pressure of that oblation, discovers that the total voluntary offering to God—offering of all his strength and all his being—is indeed his duty, a duty his free will may never refuse. Oblation could never be felt as a duty if it had not first been a fact, an irresistible impulse which human freedom may misdirect, but which it can never generate and never abolish.

Moral law, then, consists in respecting the course blindly set by the first impulse of our whole being—nothing more, nothing less. Sin sets up a resistance to this radical[3] situation, inflicting a "curve" that obliges our nature to double back upon itself, whereas sacrifice is human nature's supreme fulfillment on the level of free and conscious behavior. Sin challenges and betrays the most profound law of human nature; the love of oblation draws this nature outward into the splendor of light.

The whole law is perfectly fulfilled when our instinctive yearning to give ourselves results in oblation that is voluntary and free: the natural law and the positive Jewish law, taken in its full dimension as moral law, are merely reminders, a kind of teaching aimed at drawing Israel closer to perfect fulfillment of God's will. Even at its most exacting level, the law is not something imposed from without, destined to suffocate

men or to drive them to great efforts to surpass themselves, tearing them apart painfully. In its own way the
law only repeats the well-worn formula, "Become what
you are." And yet it sheds a piercing light on who we
are and what we have to do—freely reproduce on the
spiritual level what is being accomplished in some obscure and irresistible manner in the inaccessible depths
of our being.

Even on the Left Cheek

We can understand the second commandment only
by its similarity to the first. As long as we merely face
God out of duty or even with a love that is less than
total self-giving, it is absolutely impossible for us not to
stumble over Christ's teaching that the second commandment is like unto the first.

One observation, which really does not go into
the second commandment at great depth, gives us nevertheless an inkling of its inseparability from the first
commandment. If a man sees himself as the center of
his world—even if he tries in spite of everything to give
God the first place, the place of honor—his effort is
simply hypocritical or else despairing, and so is all effort to regard his neighbor as an equal and to render
him justice. It was partly to denounce the lie and the
impasse in which we are dragged by such efforts that
Christ made known in such concrete ways the perfection of brotherly love. If we want to love others,[4] we
must become "decentralized"; we must be projected
beyond ourselves by the love of God, at least in the
most intimate depths of our hearts where the leaven is
inserted into the dough.

Without this "decentralization," it is impossible to love one's neighbor to the very end—by offering the left cheek. Despite our sincere efforts, we shall love only those who love us and do good to those who do good to us. As for the rest of the world, while we may take part in its necessary social activities, we keep our backs carefully turned—overtly or in secret. The sick man in his bed does not expect oranges alone; he expects them to be brought out of love. Thus I maintain that without the gift-of-self demanded by the first commandment, we shall never attain the charity of the second.

Men Do Not Love Themselves

The above observation necessarily is still negative and reveals simply the impossibility of loving our neighbor as long as we do not love God more than ourselves. One can go further and discover the *positive* aspect of the two commandments by direct meditation on the love of God.

Human happiness is not at all lessened when you love God more than you love yourself. As a matter of fact those who really love have a more passionate thirst for happiness than egoists. Egoists fatally shrink their heart's desires, gradually sacrificing the joy of living to their own comfort—growing increasingly negative and petty so as to end up in a sort of euthanasia: "To sleep, perchance to dream" (Hamlet). A strange paradox, well confirmed by experience, has it that only those who give themselves entirely are able to enjoy and desire, simply because really being alive always involves running risks that no man could possibly face if he spent all his time protecting himself against invasion by others.

More profoundly, much more profoundly, do the

saints yearn for happiness. However, they love God more than they thirst for happiness, because they know that the love of God, far from quenching thirst or beating back desire, lies at the very root of that thirst and feeds it endlessly. The intense desire for happiness is harnessed by their desire to please God in the torment of his glory and the love of his holy will. Thus their appetite for living draws from the true source and is increased a thousandfold. Love of happiness pours from a wellspring of love which is infinitely greater than happiness itself, for it draws upon a more vast good and so eventually attains its full meaning, its splendor and its intensity. Only to the good in ourselves can we give absolute love; the love of ourselves must come second, for then we liberate the truth underlying all our desires, giving them free rein to express themselves in spontaneity that anticipates the kingdom of heaven.[5] As Ernest Hello wrote:

> Man does not love himself, and man should love himself a lot because he must love his neighbor—he must love him as he loves himself. If men loved themselves they would hate anything that opposes their own destiny, their needs, their joys, their light. They would hate error. They would never lose sight of paradise lost, and their horror of the serpent would lie deeper than their very breath. If men really loved themselves they would abhor with an abhorrence that is totally new every obstacle that intervenes between themselves and God.[6]

Worthy of an Infinite Love

When the second commandment asks us to love our neighbor as ourself, it obviously does not aim to put all mankind into one bag and make it the norm that each man defends all others in the same way he would defend himself. Such a view may be all right for pagans who believe that human life has no value. We must love our neighbor as ourself, but we must not love so little or so haphazardly that ours becomes an animal, instinctive love. Rather, we love ourselves because we find within an image of a sovereign being; we are able to know him and to be united with him in a manner which somehow prefigures and permits us through natural desire to suspect and see the more perfect union of grace.

Seen in this light, we do indeed merit infinite love. This love, however, is entirely subordinate to the love of the Creator, as if under the radiance of divine good. A reflector holds no light of its own and can only be measured in the dimension of the good it reflects; in this case, the good is infinite. In this light the intelligent man shows that he is worthy of being loved. The egoist and the idolater obviously love themselves less than the man who renounces the first place and who sees himself in all his poverty as necessarily relative to the Other, for this relationship contains a value that a self-centered person could never dream of.

Love of neighbor is only fully attained when we let the splendor of God, loved above all, pour forth first upon ourselves and then upon our neighbor, who will thereby come to sense something of the weight of this "love surpassing all." Thus we can understand St. John's great theme: "Little children, love one another; this is the commandment of Jesus Christ and it is enough for us if we understand it."

Sadly enough, the loftiest truths are the most easily betrayed. Loving other people means stripping ourselves of all the ties of flesh and blood, going beyond natural inclinations that shrink our spirit, avoiding all self-seeking in attachments—in other words, loving for the sake of giving, not for the sake of receiving. Here, our attitude of oblation is absolutely impossible to hold toward others if not first held toward God, because the love of God, which is a true state of true oblation, *gives* true happiness, whereas the love of neighbor does not. On the contrary, it supposes that we already have this happiness and that we are yearning to impart it.

Love for others is the test by which we recognize the presence of God within us; he who is unable to love his brother whom he sees, how can he love God whom he does not see? It is no use imagining that God can be loved by loving his "presence in other people" or that natural human love can impel a person to love God. Quite the contrary, the teaching of the Gospel requires a total break with all our natural attachments, a stripping clean to buy the precious pearl. The second commandment is like the first because it is really with the *same love*, the same outflow, the same dazzlement that we must love God and neighbor, each for the sake of God alone and in response to the same enticement. For the lure that fascinates us is the same, and it is very clearly God. Saying that the second commandment is like the first is saying that the price of spiritual man is like that of God: "How much more important you are than the birds" (Lk. 12:24).

The Light That Condemns Pity

One of revelation's most vital functions is the progressive cleansing of our eyes and our hearts, so that delivered "from the darkness that hides the malice and ugliness of sin" we may discover the wonders of the law of love. Parallel to this discovery and concurrently, we experience the deepening awareness of our agonizing inability to keep this law. The new light is difficult to accept because it condemns us before it justifies us. He who dares to look upon the splendor of an innocent nature infallibly discovers he that is no longer innocent. Only he can make this self-discovery.

It is normal that we find this difficult at the start; our sin lies in resisting when we begin to understand that this light will plunge us into an increasingly uncomfortable knowledge of self. Hard-bitten Pharisees that we are, refusing to see our own depravity, we feel obliged to repulse such perfection, to view it as inaccessible to ordinary men and women. We protest that it is something suitable only for God and for saints, and in any case something that we aren't obliged to imitate.

St. Jerome ran into this kind of betrayal of the Gospel's message. "It's quite impossible," he has told, "to love one's enemies; it's contrary to nature. The best one can do is not to hate them and to wish them no ill." Or, as we say of those with whom no reconciliation is really desired, "I have nothing against him."

Christians don't reserve this kind of special treatment just for their enemies; everyone they don't like is included, because it is "really better" to avoid such a person. All this explains a certain definition of Christian charity as "the love reserved for those one doesn't like." This non-malevolent flight from dialogue is a feeble imitation of love; admission of being incapable of doing any better is the same as an admission of being unable to love. Incapable of loving? As St. Jerome said, to be incapable of fasting or of chastity, even when it is genuine, is excusable, but there is no excuse for being incapable of loving—if it is genuine, it condemns you!

Opening the Gospel

There is nothing left but to open the Gospel and submit, as the apostles did, to the flagellation of Christ's words without muffling them quickly under soothing commentaries that elude or lessen their impact. Most people expect, and at times demand, a downy protective cloud from their preachers. To this, St. Francis of Assisi and others retorted by simply living the words of the Gospel to the letter. To take the Gospel literally involves not a materialistic interpretation but an understanding of their true spirit, the very opposite to what human tepidity puts forth as "spiritual interpretation."

The saints were crazy enough to take the Gospel "full in the face" and not merely because they *were* saints; they took it that way so they *could become* saints. They opposed the ever-prevalent notion that the Gospel in all its virulence is addressed only to a small and admirable but hardly imitable elite who just don't live like everybody else.

For example: "And as for you, do not seek what you shall eat or what you shall drink and do not exalt yourselves; for all these things the nations of the world seek and your Father knows that you need them. But seek the Kingdom of God and all these things shall be given to you besides" (Lk. 12:29-30). Can one "live in the world" and practice this wholly? Apparently not. And yet, why not? The blunt answer: because of sin— our own and the sins of others. We are afraid to hear

these truths, and so we seek nice commentaries which
empty the teaching of all substance by justifying the
secret belief that "one takes a little and leaves a little."
Such texts carefully explain that some fears and anxie-
ties are legitimate while others are not, and this is true
enough. Yet the enormous sin of greed that Christ was
condemning is passed over in silence, and so is the
enormous participation of Christians. This simple omis-
sion is enough to set up a protective shelter behind
which we tend our illicit resistance and refuse to say
"mea culpa."

War or Peace?

"Do you think that I came to give peace on earth?
No, I tell you, but division. For henceforth in one
house, five will be divided, three against two, and
two against three. They will be divided, father
against son, and son against father; mother against
daughter and daughter against mother; mother-in-
law against daughter-in-law and daughter-in-law
against mother-in-law. He who loves father or
mother more than me is not worthy of me; and he
who loves son or daughter more than me is not
worthy of me." And again: "If anyone comes to
me and does not hate his father and mother, his
wife and children, and brothers and sisters, yes and
even his own life, he cannot be my disciple" (Lk.
12:51-53; 14:26; Mt. 10:34-37).

These words are precise; they are hard. And we use
their very hardness as an excuse to surround them with
that protective cloud so that their vital impact is very

rarely felt. Brotherly love is shoved forward in their place, or else the gentleness of Christ ("Learn from me for I am gentle and humble of heart") and his promises of peace. From here on, the matter is quickly finished; those unsettling words of Jesus are rapidly blurred in the hearts of Christians who no longer care to be disturbed by such things and who label all efforts at awakening them to reality as pharisaical.

It is hard to reconcile this teaching with other aspects of the doctrine and teaching of Christ, and, of course, problems arise. Yet, in saying what he did, Christ intended those difficulties to be faced. He wanted to teach us to reach down to the depths where those difficulties could be dissolved in the strength and sweetness of the Holy Spirit, for it can only be done there. Such meditation, though austere and sometimes heart-rending, is a liberating experience. To substitute a colorless compromise with the more-or-less open intention of abolishing one of the logical results of Christian doctrine is simply to cultivate the clandestine heresy which this book seeks to expose.

In actual fact the severity of Christ's words masks a sweet and gentle secret—that of brotherly love. Obviously, this is unexpected, and yet it is easy enough to understand. Such love is so absolute, so consuming that a genuine "allergy" opposes it to the things of this world. Even the ties of flesh and blood are unable to assimilate it, or "tolerate" it, to use the medical expression. Love requires us not to judge, not to condemn, to give in good measure "pressed down, shaken, heaped up and overflowing," to struggle to enter by the narrow gate in order to attain the right frame of mind, to offer the left cheek after having been slapped on the right, not asking for the return of goods that have been taken

(Lk. 6:30)—the obligation, in fact, of praying for those who calumniate us, blessing those who curse us, plunging into the spirit of the Beatitudes to the very limit of effort. And there, this time through the movement of grace, we rejoice and exult when we are persecuted. This program is something so pure, so intense that the least softening would simply destroy it.

Love Against Love

And so, one either accepts this challenge or one does not. Of course, it one accepts, he may not really practice it, which involves another question, one to which these reflections are leading. Perhaps no one practices it *less* than those people who are always talking about "giving themselves" but who surround the notion with tasteless commentary and dilute it with human mediocrity. It is far better to be in open revolt than to betray with the kiss of Judas.

Still, there is absolutely no compromise possible between those who love and search for enlightenment (even though they know it will condemn them: "I know thy works, those are neither cold nor hot. I would thou wert cold or hot. But thou art lukewarm, and neither cold or hot. I am about to vomit thee out of my mouth"—Rev. 3:15-16) and those who go to any length to avoid it so as not to be condemned. Inevitably the wall of Yes and No goes up between them, and in the end this wall turns out to be liberating because it is revealing. If evil has to exist in this world, it is just as well that it should be revealed. "Behold, this child is destined for the fall and for the rise of many in Israel, and for a sign that shall be contradicted. And thy own soul a sword shall pierce, that the thoughts of many hearts may be revealed" (Lk. 2:34-35). Jesus did not come to bring peace but the sword, the starting point of judgment, separating those who love and those who do not want to (and within ourselves between the forces that love and those that do not). "If anyone does not hate his father, his mother, yes and *even his own* life . . ."—this judgment is pronounced, as it forever shall be, by the very ones who decide whether to love or not to love.

In this situation it is not surprising that love opposes love in an implacable struggle. On the one hand there are the things we love for our own comfort: material possessions, family, friends, reputation, and even the cherished self-images that we sometimes defend with our very lives—things that have been secretly annexed to the "me," to what St. John calls "the pride of life" ("and if I distribute all my goods to feed the poor, and if I deliver my body to be burnt, and have not charity, it profiteth me nothing"—I Cor. 13:3). And on the other hand, we have the love that loves for God's sake —in other words, the love of neighbor who is made in the image of God.

My God, I Don't Love You

Apart from the very few privileged beings who are purified, or nearly so, at their mother's breast, our road to sainthood—that is to say, our salvation—lies in the inevitable discovery of the incapacity that condemns us. "Peter, do you love me?" This is the question Jesus Christ poses to all mankind, asking that he be understood and that each of us admit that the answer is "no." This admission is the beginning of a great conversion, at the end of which each will be able to answer with Peter, "Lord, thou knowest all things; thou knowest that I love you" (Jn. 21:17).

There is no harm in making children repeat the acts of faith, hope and charity as long as they are in theological innocence and the terrible results of original sin have not yet manifested themselves. In adults these acts tend to degenerate into routine, avoiding true awareness. As a matter of fact they would be expressed far more honestly by acts of non-faith, non-hope, and non-charity. For example, listen to Marie-Noel:

> My God, I don't love you and I don't even want to, because I am bored with you. Perhaps I don't even believe in you. But look at me as you go by! Take shelter for a moment in my soul and set it in order with a breath, without seeming to, without saying anything to me. If you want me to believe in you, bring me some faith. If you want me to love you, bring me some love. As for me, I haven't any, and there is nothing I can do about it. I can only give you what I've got, my weakness and my grief. And this tenderness that torments me and that you can surely see . . . and this despair . . . this maddening shame. My pain, nothing but my pain! That's all. And my hope![8]

A Heart "Capsized" by the World's Suffering

Every time our eyes meet the eyes of our brother man, the look we intercept is that of Jesus Christ imploring us to love. It is the same with every grief-stricken face reflecting sorrow that is deepened by our indifference—"I am Jesus whom you are persecuting.

. . . For I was hungry and you did not give me to eat; I was thirsty and you gave me no drink; I was a stranger and you did not take me in; naked and you did not clothe me; sick and in prison, and you did not visit me" (Acts 9:5; Mt. 25:42-43). A certain activism has been attached to these words; they are seen as a call to social action. This is not a bad idea and yet Christ makes far higher demands: he asks for love. Love cannot remain passive, it is true, but many people plunge into social action trying to gather the fruits of love without having first planted the tree of love.

It is as dangerous for us to allow our spirits to be invaded by all the distress and thirst in the world as it is to suffer invasion by Christ; indeed it is the same thing. There are people with an authentic enough love of God who have never allowed the world's distress to upset them; their smooth-riding boat has never been capsized by the hurricane of pity. These unfortunate people will never know that in the heart of the wreckage God lies hidden, nor will they understand that the tidal wave is that very God they have sought after so hard and so long, sought even through great austerities.

The first step in the right direction is understanding that there is no outer limit to love, that love cries out: "You are wise in Christ but I am a fool in him." Much has been gained when it is possible to look upon this madness and see it as the inexorable wisdom of love, and to admit that those who remain outside this folly remain outside love.

Is This Possible for Men?

Many truly noble spirits go as far as understanding that "it is enough to love," that love is "the law and the prophets," and that loving frees us from all other obligations: "Love and do what you wish."

A great many, however, believe that they can love without much cost, and they risk becoming Pharisees because they do not really try to love. If a *real effort* is made, the result is guaranteed, and it becomes one of the surest fruits of the religious life, the search for perfection. The effort consists in a merciless, in-depth search of our own resistance to love. At times, men of good will see the need for such effort, but they still hope to reach their goal by acts of great generosity, renouncement and self-sacrifice. These are beginners, Pelagians; they are acceptable as long as they do not go too far in their illusions.

Others, by dint of trial and failure, arrive by these efforts (not entirely sterile) to the point where, upon seeing how far love can go, they realize that they are absolutely incapable of it. They recognize them in the deepest recesses of their being the presence of an infinite judge who tells them, "You do not love." St. Augustine's maxim turns against them and they flounder in a Kakfa-like universe: "If you loved, you could do as you wish; but you do not love . . . so you can still do as you wish, but you will not escape condemnation."

The Protestant churches, greatly to their credit, abound with the sort of Christian who daily lives the betrayal of Peter, which is, after all, the betrayal of every one of us. Many more people, alas, do not allow that truth to form a ripple on the calm surface of their conscience, and with desperate obstinacy they repress the voice of the infinite judge. Then, for us all, comes the wild flight through charitable and often generous undertakings; under such cover it is easier to hide the alarming proddings of conscience, proclaiming loudly that Christianity isn't as complicated as all that and that it really involves no more than giving service to others, without hunting for God-knows-what kind of spiritual "refinements" invented for those who have nothing better to do. An attitude like this is generally a poor cover-up for deep secret discontent, an anxiety complex which makes so-called open and generous religiosity stifling and tiresome for other people.[10]

Such people have no pity for themselves or for others. They refuse to listen to the voice of distress. They cannot tolerate the sight of sorrow lest their shallow benevolence be smitten with sterility. Passionately superficial (the same passion they use to defend the illusions that stop us from tumbling into the depths) they condemn us for being as superficial as they are, repudiating anything that might put them in danger of the deep. St. Peter might have been like that, had he not been caught up in his wonderful passion of folly for Jesus Christ, so that, having betrayed him, he broke down and wept.

Sooner or later, each of us must face the truth that we have betrayed love. Not accepting this truth as our daily bread leads us to spectacular collapse. Peter's denial is the most beautiful example. It should serve as a warning.

Aspirin and Dentists

Now we turn to those who have agreed to recognize themselves as sinners, guilty of the basic sin of not loving. Such people, perhaps, have ears to hear the final explanation of their failure. It is not enough to love God above all else and to love your neighbor as yourself, because God proposes something else, and consequently he demands something else.[11] The scribe who questioned Christ and who understood the law of love was "not far from the kingdom of heaven" (Mk. 12:34), but he wasn't quite there either. And those generous souls who love God and their neighbor are also not far from the Kingdom of heaven. Yet, "one thing is still lacking." On learning that there was a Savior, these souls purely and simply waited to be saved. To be sure there was nothing banal about the salvation they expected: a spiritual salvation, restitution to the state of innocence and freedom from the intolerable suffering that comes from the increasingly obscure and oppressive awareness that something is wrong, that life is a nightmare and men are made for woe.

Although Jesus Christ came to deliver us from woe, there was something far greater he wanted to give us, and this "plus" was the reason for his coming. "I have come to cast fire upon the earth, and what will I but that it be kindled?" (Lk. 12:49). There is worse yet to come, for in our wretchedness we are not only not able to love, but we have lost the "plus" about which we know nothing at all. And so it doesn't interest us precisely because we have lost it.

Most people are made aware of their human weakness when faced with pain and death. Such suffering often causes them to cry out for help. The nobler souls of whom we were speaking are driven in the same way to seek help, driven by the sheer weight of the spiritual prison they discover within themselves. And yet both types invariably seek deliverance from the *effects* of their misery, rather than from the misery itself. A doctor might say that they were demanding treatment of the symptoms rather than a true cure. As C. S. Lewis recalls:

When I was a child, I often had toothache. I knew that if I went to find my mother, she would give me something to take away the pain and I should be able to sleep. But I only went to her when the pain was really very bad. And this is why: I was sure that she would give me an aspirin, but I also knew that she would take me to the dentist the next morning. In fact, I couldn't get what I wanted from her without getting something else that I did not want. Immediate relief was not available unless I agreed to having my teeth definitely fixed. I knew the dentist well, and I knew that he would take a look at the other teeth that had not yet begun to hurt. If you give an inch to these people they will take a mile.

If you don't mind, I would like to say that Our Lord is like the dentist. Quantities of people go to him to be cured of some secret vice that they are ashamed of and that obviously spoils their daily life. Our Lord will cure them but he will not stop there. Perhaps that is all you require of him; but once you have called on him to help, he will give you the full treatment.[12]

Saved by a New Commandment

The grace of Christ then is not only—nor even primarily—a cure. If we want to content ourselves with being cured we never shall be. What is more, God never offered mankind a purely natural destiny, consisting only of loving him above all else, no matter how admirable the love may be. He proposed that men should be "consecrated" by the invasion of divine fire, and that offers quite a different perspective.

This fire was lost as a result of original sin, and the Savior came to restore it by giving us a *new* commandment: "Love one another *as* I have loved you" (Jn. 15:12). Perhaps we do not always understand the extraordinary depth of the word "as." It is generally taken here to mean "as I have loved you to the very end" ("Greater love hath no man than that he lay down his life for his friends"—Jn. 14:12); so, too, you should love one another. "If, therefore, I, the Lord and Master, have washed your feet, you also ought to wash the feet of one another. For I have given you an example, that as I have done to you, so you also should do" (Jn. 13:15-16). This is a good interpretation but it falls short. We have seen that "doing good" does not amount to loving and that we can "offer our body to be burnt" (1 Cor. 13:3) and yet have no love.

It is Christ himself who spells out the meaning of his new commandment by tying it to the context of trinitarian revelation. "As the Father has loved me, I also have loved you. Abide in my love" (Jn. 15:9). Abide, that is to say, in the Holy Spirit "that the Father will send in my name" (Jn. 14:26). It is no longer a question of innocent love—the love of the created for the Creator—but of the infinity of love, eternal, uncreated, the love given by the three persons to one another in which the human spirit is invited to abide, "that they also may be one in us, so that the world may believe that thou has sent me. And the glory that thou hast given me, I have given to them, that they may be one, even as we are one: I in them and thou in me, that they may be perfected in me, that they may be perfected in unity, and that the world may know that thou hast sent me, and that thou hast loved them even as thou has loved me" (Jn. 17:21-23).

And so we know the substance of the salvation offered by God, but we do not yet know what that means *concretely*, and so we really know nothing. Everything remains to be said about what should happen to us. At last we are ready to talk about it.

NOTES

1. C. S. Lewis, *The Problem of Pain*, p. 68.
2. Lewis, *ibid.*, pp. 50-52.
3. From which, nevertheless, it draws its existence as a vital force.
4. We cannot arrive at this by ourselves, but we may yet yearn for it with a throbbing that can grow into a veritable torment, for "the Kingdom of heaven . . . is indeed the smallest of seeds" (Mt. 13:32) and a great many forces are at war within us to hinder the flowering of the seeds of love. We can really try to be good, even though we fail continuously all along the road, on account of our human frailty. "The spirit is willing but the flesh is weak" (Mt. 26:44). Nevertheless, those who really try are by no means the same as those whose interest is so slight that they refuse to set forth along the road. "You remind me," St. Thérèse of the Child Jesus said to a novice, "of a very small child who is beginning to learn to stand up, but can't walk yet. Wishing very much to reach the top of the staircase to get to his mother, he raises his small foot to get onto the first step. The effort is useless; he keeps falling back without being able to move forward. Well then, you be that small child; by practicing all the virtues raise your small foot to climb up the staircase of saintliness, but don't ever imagine you'll be able even to make it onto that first step. No! But all the good God asks is your good will. From the top of the stairs he is watching you with love. Very soon, won over by your fruitless efforts, he will come down himself and, taking you in his arms, he will carry you off to his Kingdom, and you will never leave him again. But if

you stop raising your foot, he will leave you on earth a very long time" (*Histoire d'une âme,* complete edition, 1937, p. 261).

In the eyes of God and of the Church, there is a chasm between the *real* intention that ends in foreseen failure and the absence of all serious intention on the grounds that "it doesn't do any good." (Naturally in the eyes of the world, the chasm does not divide the effort from the absence of effort, but rather the successful efforts from the unsuccessful efforts.) There are many Christians who have accepted the total ascendency of God's love, and who groan sincerely at their powerlessness to express in action their real desire to "give their life for those they love." I do not want these Christians to be discouraged by these words which in fact are not intended for them. Nobody knows whether he is worthy of love; this is understood, but we must certainly not interpret as an absence of love the presence of forces that hold us back and prevent us from "climbing the first step."

5. But alas, only with extreme prudence can this be done here below, because, thanks to sin, we are in a state of war: "Be wise as serpents and guileless as doves" (Mt. 10:16).

6. L'Homme, *Less Alliances spirituelles,* cited by Stanislaus Fumet in "Ernst Hello ou Le Drame de la lumière," ed. Saint Michel (Paris, 1928), p. 230.

7. We should think about that when we talk about dialogue with Protestants. It should draw attention to the fact that Catholics *also* can be heretics, and frequently they are formally so in their obstinate refusal, from the bottom of their hearts, to give a real welcome to these doctrines. Protestants would probably be more ready to agree to acknowledge that the Lutheran reaction to this Catholic refusal involves a lot of secret stiffening against the plentitude of the revealed Word, if only a greater number of Catholics allowed themselves to be purged of their blindness of heart.

8. Marie-Noël, *Notes intimes,* ed. Stock, p. 41.

9. Pelagius thought our conversion depended on our freedom alone. This doctrine still smolders. A current phrase sums it up nicely: where there's a will, there's a way.

10. "If people knew all the nasty feelings that give rise to generosity, they would not make so much fuss about it . . . Mrs. So-and-So belongs to the species who lives for others;

we may recognize the others by their hunted look"—C. S. Lewis, *Tactique du Diable* (Paris: Delachaux et Niestlé, ed. 1954), p. 130.

11. It is the parable of the bad mannered guests (Lk. 14:16-24).

12. C. S. Lewis, *Mere Christianity* (London: Fontana Books, 1973), pp. 167-68.

3
Fire upon the Earth

To say that God has chosen to save us by inviting us to the banquet of trinitarian interchange is practically the same as saying that he has made us mystics and contemplatives. These two words are dangerous because they are fraught with misconception, but they are irreplaceable here because they provide concrete and therefore less compromising definitions for purely doctrinal terms regarding supernatural and trinitarian life.

At first glance, the word "mystic" suggests the "special favors" that one reads about in the lives of the saints. Even if there is a relationship between such favors (or for that matter between the little consolations that from time to time descend upon every Christian) and the deep reality of mystical life, the favors *are not* the mystical life. Mystical life is perfectly compatible with the total absence of any sense of the presence of the Christian God; it can even be unaware of the existence of such presence and not realize that it deserves to be called mystical. This was the case of the peasant whose only words for explaining his prayer to the Curé of Ars were: "I tell him and he tells me." There are many who can say even less. Enclosed by insurmountable silence, they have not the "flute" spoken of by Alfred de Vigny with which to sing to themselves and others of all the wonderful things happening to them.

Perhaps it is like the awakening of adolescent love where for a long time the teenager is unaware of what is taking place but is conscious of a strange discomfort that has no name.

What is the difference between a mystic and an ordinary Christian? Only a matter of intensity! Yet when we are invaded by trinitarian life, it is difficult not to notice that something is taking place, especially when the invasion intensifies and the flame lighted by grace really starts burning seriously. Then it is that certain words take on a special meaning: for instance, the words defining the great attributes of God, or the words of spiritual regeneration—peace, love, joy—and the words of renouncement—sacrifice, abandon, exile, yearning, desire.

It is more than probable that the feelings awakened are painful, giving one the impression of *not knowing* the reality causing them. The feeling of God's absence, especially when it is painful, is a far more sure and more solid mystical condition than the feeling of his presence. When a man is really far from God, he does not feel his absence or his presence; these notions have simply no meaning to him. The mystical state is definitely a state of desire and of desolation, maintained by deep peace and hope and by a joy that is so secret as to be quite elusive.

"All discipline seems a cause for grief and not for joy, but later it brings forth the fruit of peace and justice to those who are trained in its school" (Heb. 12:11). "How irksome she [wisdom] is to the unruly. The fool cannot abide her; she will be like a burdensome stone to test him and he will not delay in casting her aside. . . . Listen, my son, put your feet into her fetters and your neck under her yoke; stoop your shoulders and carry her and be not irked by her bonds. With all your soul, draw near to her; with your strength, keep her ways. Search her out, discover her; seek her and you will find her. Then when you have her do not let her go. Thus will you afterward find rest in her and she will become your joy" (Sir. 6:21-29).

Consolations and light, on the other hand, are contingent to the mystical state, a sort of foretaste of eternity to give a little courage and endurance to men. "If anyone wishes to follow me, let him deny himself; take up his cross daily and follow me" (Lk. 9:23). The daily cross is itself the mystical life. It is a cross so heavy that it will certainly not be accepted by those who already reject the penance of the responsibilities of everyday life and brotherly tolerance. No doubt grace gives us strength to bear grace, yet this strengthening will in itself be odious to one who has turned away from the spirit of renouncement.

The Preaching of John the Baptist

Only a church that teaches moral law is in a position to pave the way for the acceptance of grace. Mysticism becomes apparent only after a certain degree of intensity has been reached. Meanwhile, there is nothing to be done but to make an offering of oneself to the service of God and other people—that is the law of love. It must, however, be clearly understood that there are not *two* moments of spiritual life—one purely moral and the other mystical. Of course, grace, by expanding natural love, may be the real source of this love for quite a long time without manifesting its transcendence; but, as I have said, the required intensity has to be reached first. In the meantime, inviting men to serve God and their brothers is, in fact, inviting them to trinitarian love, where the leaven will work on them without their realizing it.

This kind of teaching is good only insofar as it is a preparation—like that of John the Baptist—for the more intimate teaching of Christ himself. His face and his presence must be there from the beginning without, however, going too much into the details of the mystical life (unless perhaps through the lives of the saints, where indeed portrayal is not authentic unless such details are included).

On the other hand, this preliminary teaching could be harmful if it offers nothing but purely moral Christianity, entirely sufficient in itself, that remains content to await some distant stage of mystical Christianity, problematic and not wholly desirable.

The prophets up until the coming of Christ taught along the lines of that first stage. Since the time of the incarnation, however, God has wished men to know explicitly where he was leading them—into the torrential love of the Trinity. Every *adult* Christian should know this, and he should understand that by refusing to let himself be dragged beyond the limits of natural rectitude, he will never really discover natural rectitude and he will be condemned forever to pharisaism and despair.

Starting from Where We Are

There is one big objection to all this: Should we really allow ourselves to be inundated by the tides of trinitarian life while we are still on earth? If grace is

indeed the consummation of natural love, why not post-
pone the possession of these great secrets till it is time
for heaven? There we shall contemplate the glory of the
divine fire, really tasting the flavor "that surpasses all
feeling." No doubt, the life of the Three unfolds within
the heaven of just souls as it unfolds in its own heaven
above, but here it remains a dark mystery known by
faith alone, and quite impenetrable to consciences. Apparently, then, the only thing that happens to a Christian is the rehabilitation of his innocence by grace.
Trinitarian splendors are already there but knowledge
of them is more a matter of promise than of immediate
possession, the reward for those who have done their
best, humanly speaking, and have kept the faith, "the
substance of the things hoped for" (Heb. 11:1).

This conception is certainly not that of the Church
Fathers nor is it proposed in the writings of the apostles. "Our citizenship is in heaven" (Phil. 3:20). Such
thinking too often leads to the deplorable situation
where fully mature, highly cultured persons are profoundly ignorant of Gospel revelation, displaying a dis-
armingly infantile attitude in their religious practices,
especially in matters of confession, for example. The
faith of these Christians brings nothing but constraint
to their intellect. In practice, they believe their religious
habits to be well-founded, but theirs is exactly the faith
the modernists go in for. It means adopting a filial attitude toward God the Father and praying to him as a father. What it can all mean to God is another mystery,
something "our feeble reasoning cannot hope to understand." In other words, there is nothing to understand
and one shouldn't try to understand—better just to
bend the neck piously.

This state of affairs is deplored by many pastors

who complain about the religious ignorance of their
flocks. Maybe they expect too much or too little. Simple souls are not always as apt to profit from theological,
biblical, patristic or liturgical formation as might be
supposed. What really matters is the quantity of light
that has been absorbed rather than an abundance of
secondary knowledge. In this respect priests, distrustful
of the mystical life, frequently fail to go far enough in
their reaction to the ignorance of Christians. They are
desperately eager to provide a sound religious formation on humanistic lines, but they are content to leave
the deeper illumination of God to the great beyond.
They proffer abundant nourishment on the revealed
mysteries, but the mysteries themselves are not introduced, for these good pastors do not in fact believe
that their sheep are called to enjoy such tasty fare. To
the mystics they apply the same treatment as Descartes
applied to theologians: they are supermen, admirable
but not imitable, special kinds of beings who manage to
penetrate into the sanctuary by some weird kind of bur-
glary which at best is the result of charisma, and, at
worst, mental illness.

    In this area, the rupture that started with the Re-
naissance has not yet been repaired. The many fervent
and respected spiritual movements that were born during the 17th century and perhaps too closely tied to the
mentality of their day were swept away during the
French Revolution. The spiritual movements of the
19th century leave a terribly negative impression of
being a defense reaction rather than a return to a grand
tradition. Only the great saints—the Curé of Ars, for
instance—escaped from the limitation of that century;
they stand like solitary prophets in a world more and
more empty of God.[7]

Thérèse and the Return to Sources

It was then necessary to await Thérèse of Lisieux to again discover a spirituality with dimensions as vast as the Gospel. This child of shepherds, not of kings, tore herself instinctively from the heresies that over the centuries had come between mankind and the Gospel. She plunged unhesitatingly into the spring of living water promised by Jesus to those who believe in him, the spring that nourished the contemplation of Paul and John and the dawning Church.

Her originality lay not so much in rediscovery as in her refusal to seek anywhere else: "For I am determined not to know anything among you except Jesus Christ and him crucified" (1 Cor. 2:2). In the midst of a world grown more and more eccentric, hers was the mission to erect the standard of evangelical simplicity for shepherds and kings to gather around, avid for light and for love and for reality, as they had gathered around the manger of Bethlehem. Thérèse, without knowing the meaning of the word "modernism," was fully modern. Indeed, she was diametrically opposed to modernism, for she was royally indifferent to the more-or-less reactionary or humanistic values her contemporaries were using to bolster "religion" and to counteract "the new trends." She did not waste her time on the sad struggles that exhausted the clergy. From the very start she took her stand on the spot where St. Augustine had said earthly cities must crumble—in eternity. For her, as for Augustine and for all the Church Fathers, eternity had already begun.

A great deal has been said about return to the sources and not chopping the life out of the Gospel. But since we are so obstinately intent on shunting into the next world that burning intrusion of trinitarian life which is the Gospel, and since the divine fire is not supposed to invade the human, there is nothing left but for the human to invade the divine, breathing life into our adherence to Christ by offering all the world's vitality to him in homage. Surely this is a return to the perspectives of purely natural law. Between love of life and fear of life, we must resolutely choose love; this is obvious. But for anyone wanting to live, there were not three ways out. Either one must chose to live the life of the world or else the life of Christ which is interior and hidden—and that means mystical—or nothing at all. To reserve this mystical life for a special category of so-called elite Christians and not to offer it freely to all, to distrust the very desire for it because of the deviations it might entail (one might as well distrust the Gospel on account of possible heresies), is nothing but a betrayal of the Gospel. It sets the stage for a betrayal of Christ himself through re-enactment of Peter's treachery.

The Look Returned; Washing of the Feet

Even fiercer resistance is offered by some people to the word "contemplative." Contemplation is held to be some kind of Greek refinement in direct opposition to the Christian spirit. As this book does not propose to go into that dispute, it will be enough to remember why it is that Christian contemplation is not a philosophical exercise. Christian contemplation is trinitarian—two looks of fire being consumed by love. Our contemplation is not our own, but God's, the same God who by the Holy Spirit is searching for us through the face of Christ. God does this and nothing else, and we have nothing else to do either except to swing gently and progressively into this eternal contemplation. This is the very precise meaning given to the word "contemplative"; it implies a dialogue, and it refers to the interior life of God and to *all* Christian life.

What is a dialogue? The word and the reality are fashionable today. Perhaps this is a good thing, though one is inclined to wonder whether the full depth of meaning is always understood. "Dialogue" tends to be used for a simple exchange of words, crossing one another, where each person makes his contribution. However, the quantity of words is not the important thing. Real dialogue is something far deeper; it consists of a single person speaking *on behalf of* another who is listening with all his soul and "keeping the words in his heart." Music, for example, is a far more satisfying dialogue than lengthy discussion. When a violin is played for someone special, the exchange becomes infinitely precious between the one who plays and the one who listens. The listener contributes as much as the musician. His silence is not inert, and it is the only answer that is perfectly right. The perfect answer to intimate confidences is found only in silence.

No matter how important our occupation, we have only one destiny, even here on earth, and that is to allow ourselves to be progressively consumed by the exchange, the dialogue that comes from God and returns to God. To the extent that a Christian accepts prayer, he understands this fact. He does not pray in order to modify or change the will of God (for that is impossible) but to comply with God's deep intention of dialogue with man. This is the one thing that God is unable to do alone, for dialogue requires two. A prayer that escapes from the routine wants, the obsession with temporal results, a prayer that seeks for Christ like someone who would come face to face with Someone—such prayer, consciously or not, is contemplative.

What then is the meaning for Christians of loving our brothers? It means to desire this dialogue for him as much as we desire it for ourselves. This is the supreme aim of all human activity: to give life to children of God, to nourish them, clothe them, instruct them; to allow them to expand and to bring them to full flower that God in his turn may offer them his love.[8]

Following the example of Christ, we must wash one another's feet, first of all as a material duty (and this includes every imaginable form of charity), but above all to sing of God's desire to wash our feet. And this can only mean contemplative intimacy. Faith and hope may pass away, but that act of love will remain forever, and so will the action of Mary Magdalene who poured her tears over the feet of Jesus, and perfume of great price upon his head, perfume that "might have been sold" for the poor (Mk. 14:5). For the poor, money perhaps, but not love—and as for Mary, "wherever in the whole world this Gospel is preached, this also that she hath done shall be told in memory of her" (Mk. 14:9).[9]

All activity of this nature is fundamentally heavenly, and therefore contemplative, and all else we must do as though not doing it, "for this world as we see it is passing away, but our citizenship is in heaven" (1 Cor. 7:31; Phil. 3:20).

Fire upon the Earth

Whoever tries to love not only those who please him but also his enemies, not by merely doing them good but in the unending torment of trying to catch their eyes so as to give them *everything* in dialogue, is, perhaps even unknown to himself, a contemplative. A mother's devotion to her child would lose all significance if over and beyond the numerous daily tasks, her maternal love did not oblige her to gaze deeply into the eyes of her child—such action is the property of love. So, too, husband and wife both work to support the family, and probably love is expressed by this work, yet love seeks something more in an intimate dialogue between those who love one another.

Whoever does not act thus, who spends his strength without giving himself, without accepting the surrender of self in the eternal dialogue which begins here upon earth, is not a Christian, or at any rate he does not act like one. I must stress that this dialogue with neighbor, just like the dialogue with God from which it overflows, unfolds in the dark austerity of faith. We are, in fact, looking toward that which is invisible to us, and we are living for the things that are not seen (2 Cor. 4:18). That is what makes us Christians, that is to say, contemplatives. What we are has not yet been revealed to us, but we carry this treasure in vessels of clay. Yet where our treasure is, there our hearts also are (1 Jn. 2:3; 2 Cor. 4:7; Lk. 12:34), that is, in the invisible Kingdom of those who believe, who hope and who love.

Cauterized by Fire

Those who try to enclose Christian life within the limits of this world throw up a last rampart against the invasion of divine fire. To be sure, they will admit in theory that such fire might make an appearance before death; they may even admit that Jesus intended it to be so. Since, however, they are in no hurry to embark upon such a program, they will distinguish two moments in spiritual life. First comes the curing of sinful nature, with the help, of course, of God and a plunge into the blood of Christ. And then there will be time enough to let themselves be initiated into the divine— later after balance has been established and the narrow way found. After all, isn't this what Christ meant when he said, "Good and faithful servant, you have been faithful over little things; I shall give you authority over many. Enter into the joy of your master" (Lk. 19:19)?

These so-called Christians interpret "little things" as referring to moral life, the seven years with Leah preceding union with Rachel (Gn. 29:16-30). They seem to believe that man must be restored to his primitive integrity before he needs to start worrying about divine things; the divine in this case is not relegated to the afterlife but postponed to await the healing of sinful nature.

Such pastoral philosophy and teaching might be translated by the maxim: "First be a man. Later become a saint. Learn to possess yourself before you presume to give yourself. You can only give what you have first conquered." Religious teaching like this is either nourished by secret idolatry in regard to human values or else by a kind of despair in the face of human deficiencies. Feeling unworthy of God's presence within, one dissociates the healing grace which is intensely desired from divine grace of which one is dumbly afraid. It is the same old story of the aspirin and the dentist. We consent to have recourse to give in proportion to our own wretchedness as we discover that we are not worth very much. And we tend to define grace as "*help*" to assist and heal our nature rather than as the fire that makes it divine.

And so it is that by all kinds of more or less tortuous ways we always arrive at the same place: grace is subordinated to nature. The truth of the matter is that grace is not at the service of nature but that nature is at the service—is made for—grace. Turning these values upside down is simply falling back into the old, everlasting, dreary monotony of Israelite idolatry. There is no healing grace apart from sanctifying grace,[11] and it is useless to try to return sanctifying grace to the Giver, as though it were too big a gift and one of which we are unworthy. Healing grace is radically trinitarian, a derivation, or rather a limited aspect of sanctifying grace. In short, God knows only one remedy for human nature—cauterization by fire.

Everyone, All at Once

The intrepid genius of Thérèse of the Child Jesus supplies a practical conclusion to this doctrine. In fact, it is one of the essentials of her message: there are not two moments of spiritual life—one of healing, purification and ascesis, and the other a remote moment of divinization, so remote in the opinion of some as to be relegated to the next world. It is certainly not a question of man coming first (with the grace of God), and then, only after man, the supreme consecration of his supernatural life, as though it were a reward for a whole lifetime of hard effort and mortification. St. Thérèse intuitively maintained that all souls, no matter what their condition may be, are *immediately* qualified to be consumed by the fires of mercy:

In the older days, only pure and spotless offerings were acceptable to a strong, all-powerful God. Victims had to be perfect in order to satisfy divine *justice* but now the law of love has replaced the law of fear . . . in order that love may be fully satisfied, we must be humble to the point of annihilation, and then love will transform this annihilation into fire."[13]

To all those who want to try *something else*, no matter what it may be, the following words are addressed. If their hesitation is caused by attachment to human values, Jesus answers them with the parable of the guests who were in no hurry to reach heaven. To those who are afraid of being unworthy, who ask for a little more time to wash up before appearing at the banquet or to learn self-control before trying to give themselves, St. Thérèse replies that "the fire of love is more purifying than the fire of purgatory."[14] Theology caps this by proclaiming that the fires of purgatory are nothing but the fire of love in the process of encountering resistance in the human soul. Thérèse continues:

If all the weak, imperfect souls should feel what the littlest of them all feels, not a single one would despair of reaching the summit of the mountain of love, since all Jesus asks for is abandonment of self and gratitude, not heroic actions."

We must all go as far as Thérèse or be guilty of resisting the Gospel's message of divine mercy: "It is not the healthy who need a physician but those who are sick. I have not come to call the just, but sinners" (Mk. 2:17).

Everybody agrees that mercy does not reject sinners and that it even solicits them, yet only the most exceptional Christian will admit that this mercy is meant for everyone, all at once, and not just those who walk in the footsteps of the workers who started in the first house or of the elder son in the parable of the prodigal.

Of course, everyone will also agree that the gifts of God are free and unforeseeable. We recognize this and so do those who are pleased to see in it a case of exceptional treatment, claiming that "God can do anything he likes, but as a general rule and so on and so on. . . ." Well, there really is a general rule, and it is this: "When his heart is moved," he opens wide the door, without any restrictions, setting no limits but the capacity of the soul (as a stomach long empty but slowly nourished), placing no barrier on his side to the infinity of his love, because that is the instinct of love, that or nothing: "Amen I say to you, this day you will be with me in paradise" (Lk. 23:43).

God knows that nothing can save us except the gift of everything and the invitation to us to love him. He invites us, in fact, to be mystics before we are men of virtue.[16] God has never allowed man to be content with just being human; the first sin was committed not against the law but against grace.[17] As a consequence of his sin, man lost his natural rectitude of spirit, and the loss of control over his passion was his punishment. By making one simple gesture, the acceptance of supernatural life that was lost by our first parents, we may recuperate *everything* in the order in which we lost it all. First comes grace, then at once, and because of grace, rectitude and will power. Next, under the impetus of the return of the sovereign good, we set out on the slow, painful reconquest of our moral strength. And then, last of all, the final enemy, death, is vanquished (1 Cor. 15:25).

Anyone trying to modify this program by aiming

at natural rectitude before offering himself to mystical
life will never even become upright. A program that can
be summed up as "Have faith and be generous" is ex-
cellent only if the definition includes the unreserved acceptance of grace. The theological meaning of grace is
not always clear to beginners, especially children. If,
however, the program offered implies the persistence of
sins as a means of self-development toward being engulfed by God, it is a condemnation of those who ad-
vertise it because it can not be put into practice. Calling
upon the name of Jesus Christ is not sufficient to obtain
his salvation: "Not everyone who says to me 'Lord,
Lord' shall enter the kingdom of heaven . . ." (not
those who obstinately persist in trying to find a way
other than trinitarian life, the only concrete offer made
by Jesus) ". . . but only he who does the will of my
Father." The will of the Father is that we be gradually
engulfed by the heart of Christ. "I am the vine and you
are the branches. He who abides in me and I in him, he
bears much fruit; for without me you can do nothing.
. . . As the Father has loved me, I also have loved you.
Abide in me" (Jn. 15:5-9). We shall be trinitarian or we
shall be nothing: trinitarian, saved, beatified in the
darkness, adopted and possessed by infinite love *before*
we become fully men, before we regain our balance as
human beings, before being pure and straight.

The Spirit of Childhood

"I praise thee, Father, Lord of heaven and earth,
that thou has hidden these things from the wise and
prudent and have revealed them to the little ones" (Lk.
10:21; Mt. 11:25). There is no need to look any further
for the root of our difficulties in receiving as we should

the revelation of the Kingdom. Our search has led us far enough—the words stressed by Christ contain unfathomable depths. Only the hearts of children are able to receive the Kingdom, and we haven't or rather we no longer have the hearts of children. God is a great child, an infinite child, and he can only live with children. If we are no longer children, we must become so. And this is like death, whose vicissitudes we shall consider, for what Nicodemus said is quite true. A man "must enter a second time into his mother's womb and be born again" (Jn. 3:4).

The spirit of childhood is trinitarian as well. This is no childishness, but the words of Jesus echoing through eternity, "Abba, Father." Does this mean that our own childhood is in question and that we must repudiate it before we can become fully adult? Certainly not! We cannot escape youthful imperfections by running away from them, or from the nostalgia of happiness lost.[18] Rather, we must go on to the very end, following the glimpse we caught in our youth. Marcel Proust said, "The cure for dreaming is not less dreaming but more dreaming. It is the whole of dreaming." The capacity for dreaming is typical of childhood. We must all follow our wildest dreams before we are able to welcome the Kingdom of heaven which surpasses all dreams. We shall never get there by despising the spirit that dreams in us, but rather by recognizing the limits of our imagination. Thus, we may learn to thirst for the greater and more real splendor which surpasses the reality in whose name we have been dreaming.

Capacity So Easily Lost

The child's heart is untamable, and it refuses to

live below a certain level of magnificence. The Gospel does not ask the child to go backward, to renounce his infinite horizons, to reconcile himself with the grey monotony of iron realities. Rather, he is asked to tear himself from all the mediocrities that still trail around in his dreams and to desire far more than "anything the heart can conceive."

Through the dreams of childhood and beyond them lies the first presentiment of the Kingdom. The trail is there, and we must follow it to the very end to leave the visible world, to soar over the invisible world with a heart that is solid in faith.

When Jesus Christ said "Let the little children come unto me," he did not mean cold saints but real flesh-and-blood children with all the faults that made St. Augustine shudder[19]—children with the deep impulse of love and the sheer joy of life that are hidden under the artless simplicity of the early years. A child meeting up with things for the first time, things like life, water, and light, is always in a state of wonder, and he is right, for he sees things as they really are. The torment of poets is nothing other than this search for wonderment that is so easily and so definitively lost by adults.

Greed is the dry wind that parches the adult. Desire to possess kills wonder. Collectivities, doctrines, mystiques that set out to conquer the world—these are what prematurely age the human heart and render it incapable of seeing the virginal and the immaculate, the poverty and splendid audacity of things. Gone is the capacity for knowing that things by their ineffable dependence on the Creator are marvelous. The eye of the child cannot be turned from God; it sees a splendor that is only apparent to eyes untouched by all covetousness.

Only he who has renounced the world possesses the precious jewel of eternal life. And only he who possesses this jewel knows how marvelous is the world he has renounced and how worthy of love, because he alone has set the world in its proper place and has received a thousand times the value of the lie he has renounced. It is not a question of setting the joys of this world in opposition to the joys of heaven, because God reveals the true joy of his creation only to those who have given him their heart. It is instead necessary, with St. Paul, to see the opposition between those who seem to have nothing and have everything and those who want to have everything and have nothing. He who wants to save his soul will lose it by losing God, and he who loses his soul will find it and all the world with it, because in the wonderment of innocence he sees the Creator even in the least of creatures.

Adults lose their capacity for joy—the true sadness of the world is as hidden from them as is its beauty. We are not able to exult as Jesus did over the smallest ray of light, the least lily in the field arrayed by the Father, or the birds of the sky receiving their nourishment. Neither can we groan or suffer over a tiny injustice as though it were an agonizing thorn in the flesh, as we should also suffer over the least lie or impiety anywhere on earth. It is necessary that evil press upon our nerves and our sensibilities before we commence to tremble; we are unaware of that shuddering of soul that drove St. Dominic to cry out: "But what will become of sinners?" We stand insensible and stupefied, surrounded by fearful and marvelous reality. Our spiritual life is one long awakening, a series of annunciations tearing us from insensibility, revealing to us little by little that which really is the splendor of God and the horror of evil.

Like a Drunken Boat

To become a child is to accept loss of footing. Without shipwreck, there is no entering into the light of God. A fearful event—St. John of the Cross has well described its horrors—but if we can be supple we have a better chance of coming through. It is a good idea to get used to *not knowing*, to knowing nothing at all, rather than to cling to the illusion of knowing something. We must approach the Kingdom in a "relaxed" frame of mind with no preconceived ideas and no fixed program set in advance. Such lack of preparation is intolerable to sages or to activists, but it is delightful to the spectator listening for the three knocks before the curtain rises, and it is a delight to a child. Only a child allows himself to be swept joyfully toward the unknown precisely because it is unknown. A child believes that everything is marvelous, especially what he does not understand, because there is wonder in his heart. And here is the secret of the ease with which the saints move around in the darkness of faith.

Obviously, then, no limit should be set to the distance and the swiftness by which the Holy Spirit will draw us, and this is also a sign of childhood. Either children have confidence or they haven't. When they have it ("I know whom I have believed"—2 Tim. 1:2), they will follow anywhere. No experience frightens them as they abandon themselves to perpetual delight. Such is the image of "abandonment" so little understood by adults. Perhaps the words of a mother describe it a little better:

> I had two children, one seven and the other four, and I played with them by hanging onto their fists and whirling them around. The little one always loved the game, but the older said one day, "Don't whirl me any faster than I want to go." This one was no longer a child.

Such a confident attitude supposes an intimate and obscure knowledge—analogous to that of a baby and his mother—of One who escorts us as we lose our footing—in other words, Jesus Christ, This knowledge rests upon a personal encounter, as we shall discuss later. To reach such abandonment, our encounter with Christ should be along the lines of his encounter with his mother. It is strange (but inevitable) that Christians who believe they can do without Mary never discover the connection between the spirit of childhood and the presence of a mother. This is just another example of the kind of sign that, because it is so very obvious, is hidden from the wise and the intelligent.

We must consent to be thrown off course, to be broken up and cut loose. One by one the road maps so carefully collected must vanish (even the one that leads up Mount Carmel). These are the conditions we must accept before we can be carried away by God into the land where there are no roads.[20] It is a question really of being in "over our heads" in the great waters of trinitarian life. And if we do not want to go as far as that, we inevitably turn also from the natural uprightness which is so dear to our hearts: "From him

who has not shall be taken even that which he has"
(Lk. 19:36).

Toward the Struggle of Jacob

Giving advice is useless until all of the angles of a
situation have been explored. This is what was wrong
with the manuals of perfection over which St. Thérèse
racked her brains; these texts are too brief and at the
same time too complex. Too brief because they over-
look the subtleties of the battle against the powers of
darkness in which we are engaged, as also those of the
ways of mercy, blazing trails through the hearts of men
through sin itself, awakening the good seed in the midst
of the weeds, and writing straight with crooked lines.
Too complex because Christian perfection consists in
simply allowing trinitarian life to breathe within us instead of suffocating in our hearts of stone. We do not
learn to breathe from anatomical and physiological
textbooks but just by breathing.

To accord with the heart of St. Thérèse, a manual
of perfection, intended to serve as a dogmatic under-
scoring of her message, would obviously have to touch
first of all on the mystery of the Holy Trinity as found
in Christian tradition. Next would come the manner in
which trinitarian life is communicated to us and what it
contains of grace and glory. These points having been
clarified as far as possible, we should then have to look
into the matter of grace to discover the nuances adopted by trinitarian life as we live it here on earth. This is
the *religious* aspect of adoration, the total oblation and
ecstasy which is not itself in God but which does adapt

certain perfections of trinitarian life to our level of being.

Then would come the manner in which this life might be lived in the darkness of faith before it unfolds into light; this is a great trial for all, a time of testing, which is brought to a triumphant conclusion by the Holy Spirit—that is to say once again, by trinitarian life. It is not a question of taking a test *on completion of which* we enter into intimacy with God. Rather the test consists in *remaining* within this intimacy ("Abide in my love") and not triumphing in some preliminary exam extrinsic to the joy of God, in order to win the right to enter into that joy. This is the reason why I am allowing myself to present the testing of faith as a new gradation of trinitarian life as it is lived by us human beings.

Because man initially failed this test, sin entered the world, and trinitarian life was extinguished in his spirit, asphyxiated by his free will. This sin was not entirely intentional and so it is reparable. A happy weakness in human will power peculiar to the nature of man, a capacity for *redemption and salvation*, followed by conversion. A strange phenomenon more wonderful than the spectacle of a world for whose beauty God allowed evil and suffered the cross—the splendor of a heart of stone which allows itself to be touched that it may begin to beat—burning what it adores and adoring what it burns. "Because my son was dead and has come to life again; he was lost and is found" (Lk. 15:24).

The mystery of the incarnation only takes on its full depth when it is again placed in the perspective of those events which so touched the heart of God. Trinitarian life in the Word Incarnate never had to go undergo the test of faith, Christ having been conceived in the vision of God face to face. Yet trinitarian life underwent another "transformation" which was achieved in the plentitude of the person of Christ and shared with Christians—the encounter with sin in that same person. Not that Jesus Christ sinned, but he allowed sin to oppress and persecute the trinitarian life in his own person to the very point of death followed by resurrection. From that time on, trinitarian life can persecute sin within the hearts of men and slay it.

These struggles together constitute the mystery of the cross and redemption, and we can see that it has to be defined as a new gradation of divine life, be it the cross of Christ or our own. All this should be analyzed in the order that I have given it so that a meditation on Christian life may be complete and result in really practical conclusions.

Such a study is obviously too wide for this little book. There is, however, a delightful figure in the Bible who personifies the combat of redemption: Jacob in his combat with the angel. I intend to dwell a little on this episode in the hope of helping Christians to understand more of what is happening to them. The one great rule of progress is learning to become reconciled to things *as they are.* God unfolds them little by little, allowing the light of love very gently to displace the dark.

It has often been said that understanding without practice is not enough. Thérèse herself said, "I don't always practice what I have understood." There is, in fact, an intensity of vision that inevitably demands passionate effort, either for action or for flight. It is possible to understand without carrying out, as long as comprehension remains more verbal than real, which is as much, really, as saying: as long as one does not understand. On the day when light dawns in all its purity, there is nothing but flight or capitulation. Only the Holy Spirit is able to present that light, but since he uses the language of revelation to introduce it, I would like to give some comment on this unveiling which, like a messenger of peace, brings us deliverance.

NOTES

1. "In the midst of life, we are in death." St. Thomas, the impassive one, could never sing this antiphon in Compline (sung by the Dominicans during Lent) without bursting into tears.

2. If the end of Chapter 2 has been properly understood, one must consider as equivalents the following terms: sanctifying grace—trinitarian life—supernatural life.

3. St. Thérèse of the Child Jesus made the refutation of this error one of her principal combats.

4. The concept, taken at its worst, discredits not only the mystical life but all Christian teaching as activity more fitting for heaven than for earth, since the latter also implies an invasion of our intelligence by eternal Light. Such teaching, of course, has a human aspect which brings it closer to this world's activities, whereas mystical life carries us to the outermost limits of the human condition. Thus, the position cited constitutes at its most virulent an attack on the great doctrinal tradition of the Church, while in its watered-down form, by far the most common, it attacks only the mystical life. The latter appears more coarse than any other optic; not content with being *officially* divine, it is really and concretely so—and for men, the *way* is more important than the substance. Marcel Proust remarked that the classicists preferred to hear modern thinkers praised by an academician than to hear Racine praised by Claudel (who had not yet become a classical writer). In the same way, human talk about the mystical life is acceptable whereas mystical talk about human affairs is not. Generally speaking, we shall be forgiven for being revolutionaries, as long as we do it in the same way as everybody else.

5. In which Christians are faithful followers of Descartes and Spinoza who maintained that the life of everyday people should develop in relation to science, independent of all religious influence. For these thinkers, faith is nothing but adherence to a light whose effective intrusion is not for this world. Exceptions are always made for a few specialists, "men who are more than men," the theologians whom Descartes smothers in respect the quicker to drive them from the city. "The work of philosophy is the search for truth; the work of faith is nothing but obedience to piety" (Spinoza). It is thus only natural, albeit deplorable, that the faithful are expected to practice obedience and piety especially in regard to those difficult questions that torment the consciences of lay people. We have drifted far from the violence with which St. Paul and the Church Fathers protested their faith and nourished it.

6. That is to say a specialty, a gift like that possessed by musicians and surgeons.

7. I would remind anyone who is tempted to think I am a pessimist of two passages in the Gospel: "And because iniquity will abound, the charity of many will grow cold" (Mt. 24:12); "Yet when the Son of Man comes, do you think he will find faith on the earth?" (Lk. 18:8).

8. In this we are widely separated from the Hindu religions for whom life, starting here below, holds no interest except as a time of testing, an opportunity offered to the soul to intensify its evolution—like some kind of play that only serves as a means of training the actors, and which here consists of turning every event into an occasion for learning detachment from everything. In short the meaning of life is detachment from life in favor of an inexpressible beyond. To be sure, there is here a truth of the greatest importance, one that has been proclaimed throughout revelation: "They are strangers and pilgrims here on earth. . . . They seek after a better, that is, a heavenly, country" (Heb. 13:16). Yet the same revelation also teaches the great importance of earthly life, the only means of bringing into being and teaching the children of God. Without social life and all it implies, heaven could never be populated, nor the mystical body brought to completion according to the order established by God.

9. This action is taken up by the Little Brothers of the Poor when they present a diamond to old couples celebrating

their diamond wedding, and it is as much criticized as was the action of Mary Magdalene.

10. The quarrels over grace in the 17th century, quarrels that were in reality concerning divine aid—*de auxiliis*—helped to fix this idea in Christian minds.

11. Cf. the text to which note 2 refers in Chapter 1.

12. Of course, there is a baptism, the "bath" purifying us in the blood of Jesus, but here the blood is just a channel of the Spirit, and all efficient baptism in the New Covenant is in reality a baptism of fire.

13. *Manuscrits autobiographiques*; col. *Livre de vie*, p. 227.

14. *Ibid.*, pp. 208 and 219.

15. "So there is question not of him who wills nor of him who runs, but of God showing mercy" (Rom. 9:16).

16. Cf. the section "Aspirin and Dentists" in Chapter 2.

17. See note 11 above.

18. The most unhappy childhood, brushed by a memory with the concrete flavor so admirably analyzed by Proust, still leaves in the heart an impression of paradise lost. It is not the events, perhaps painful, that we yearn for, then; it is for ourselves, for what we used to be. That is what we have lost beyond recall now and what seems to have been paradise.

19. In the *Confessions* (beginning).

20. Certainly, it is the catastrophic mistake of Quietism to believe oneself dispensed from the roads before God himself has abolished them. This is no reason for ignoring the less grave but more common fault of refusal to enter there where the road leads, on account of attachment to the road itself. At each transition, each metamorphosis, each "passing by" of Christ, we have to accept being for a moment like the drunken boat without map or compass: "I no longer felt the tug of the towline." We must not *wish* for this situation for ourselves (it would mean we are trying to control, which is precisely the poison of Quietism), but we must expect it and be ready for it ahead of time by drawing as closely as possible to the frank and fervent suppleness of a child's heart.

21. Modern exegetes doubt this. We do not agree with them on this point, but this is not the place to discuss it.

4

The Struggle of Jacob

But Jacob himself remained behind all alone. Then some man wrestled with him until the break of dawn. When he saw that he could not overcome Jacob, he touched the socket of Jacob's thigh so that it dislocated while Jacob was wrestling with him. Then he said, "Let me go; it is dawn." But Jacob answered: "I will not let you go until you bless me." Then he asked Jacob, "What is your name?" He said, "You shall no longer be called Jacob but Israel, because you have contended with God and men, and have triumphed." So Jacob asked, "What is your name?" He answered, "Why do you ask my name?" but he blessed him there. Jacob named the place Phanuel, saying, "I have seen a heavenly being face to face and yet my life has been spared." The sun rose on him just as he left Phanuel, limping because of his thigh (Genesis 32:25-32).

This text is as deep as eternity.

"Some man . . ." Who is this man? In the end we find out that he is God himself in the form of a messenger, an "angel." Tradition has handed down the word "angel," but it risks leading us into error. The man in question actually is God, since Jacob is astonished that he has seen him and still remained alive.

True, it happened at night, and the man did ask that he might depart, for "it is dawn," as though he could not allow his face to be seen in broad daylight. None of that is said; it is only suggested in a kind of savage, silent modesty. The words exchanged are so terrifyingly intense, with a tenderness so secret that it would be unbearable to describe them in lyrical language. It is a combat of love, yet the word is never spoken. It involves God, but this is not said until the very end. This, by the way, is quite a specialty of Jacob's—this finding out when it is all over that "Yahweh was there and he had known" and then being afraid in retrospect, or, like the disciples at Emmaus, joyous in retrospect.

Why did it happen at night? Because Jacob's face-to-face encounter was not that of heaven, and the night protected him from God's intolerable glory, even as the hand of the Lord protected Moses. This is also why the combat is really an image of our life, which is indeed a long night that very gradually gives place to the dawn of eternal life.

Is God Powerless?

"When he saw that he could not overcome . . ." —by these simple words we are swept into the depths of the secret of God. God cannot conquer man!

In the first chapter, we learned that our identity is revealed to us as our worship of God deepens. The fearful corollary of this is our awareness of our liberty and above all the respect God has for this liberty. Here we touch on what is both the most precious and the most vulnerable part of revelation. The most precious, because we are faced *concretely* with the depths of God's love, and we had never imagined its force and its delicacy. The most vulnerable, because, like all great love, it is timid and yet totally possessive. It gives all and demands all, but it respects our liberty, scorning the sort of seduction that would diminish its own light by "drugging" us, if I may use the word, with some enticement other than God himself known in his truth. This great love is not timid even though total, but rather timid because it is total. It is precisely because it desires everything that it leaves us free to use our awesome freedom and to refuse if we so choose.

It is here that God's respect for us becomes so formidable, because it involves what theologians call the permission to sin, and all the consequences that sin entails. If the infinite delicacy of God really allows us the liberty of saying no to him, he has to permit us to say no for always. A provisional no is not really a no, unless there is a secret understanding that the provisional not be prolonged indefinitely.

The time for unleashing the wicked word is at hand; the danger of going to hell is connected with this notion of respect. This danger would be unreal if hell were not real, or if, as is so often proposed, there were no one in it. And if indeed this danger were unreal, then Jesus Christ was scaring the women of Jerusalem for the fun of it when he said: "For if in the case of green wood they do these things, what is to happen to the dry?" (Lk. 23:31). If there were no hell, the cross would be so much play-acting and the Gospel would be an empty tale, and so would be the very love of God for man.

It is blasphemy to minimize the catastrophe from which mankind has been saved at the price of the Savior's blood. Unconsciously, even the best of men glide from time to time into the illusion that there is no hell. And yet how frequently has Christ taken the trouble to appear to certain saints that he might dispel this dangerous illusion. He appeared, for example, to Angela de Foligno: "My love for you is not merely a joke," and to Margaret Mary: "Look at this heart that has so loved mankind, though in return it has received nothing but contempt and ingratitude."

The cross as well as the warning of Jesus Christ teaches us that if there is a struggle, sacred and blessed, with the grace of God (struggle on which we are meditating at the moment), there also exists a most effective and dangerous resistance which takes the form of refusing struggle—in the military sense of the expression—by avoiding the encounter. It is before this invincible flight from battle that God bows when he renounces all efforts to save us.

This does not mean that those who do give battle avoid grave sins, that is, avoid the state of sin behind which our souls take shelter as though within a fortress. Nevertheless, in spite of everything, perhaps even without our knowing, something within us calls out to the Liberator, and, in so doing, calls for the battle that must follow. This already is a beginning, though in sin, of the interior division denounced by St. Paul: "I feel two men within me" (cf. Rom. 7:14-25).

It is very difficult, as a matter of fact, to distinguish between those who are hewn into a block with their sin (sometimes almost imperceptible and apparently not too grave) and who present smooth, well-greased walls as an unassailable front to the grace of

God, and those who in the depths of their hearts hide a secret fissure through which the breath of the Holy Spirit can pass unrecognized, causing dissatisfaction, yearning, hunger, the constant reoccurrence of the same faults and all the symptoms that betray the soul's disarray. Yet by these signs one may know that the great battle has begun.

A Heart at Rest; An Intellect in Distress

Dismaying though this outlook may be, it has an even more formidable aspect—that of the purity of our faith. Faced with these mysteries, our intellect suffers more keenly than our heart. For to all those who are terrified by hell, God offers the merciful refuge of the murmur of the One who is gentle and humble of heart: "Come to me, all you who labor and are overburdened, and I will give you rest" (Mt. 11:28). These may also hear the message of St. Thérèse of the Child Jesus because it is for them that she speaks and for them that God sent her to earth. And they are also the ones able to penetrate into the mystery of the Holy Virgin and to learn to feel something of the infinitely tender Wisdom who made of his mother both the Immaculate Conception and the refuge of sinners.

Distress of heart has nothing to fear from the Christian message, which is entirely one of hope for those in despair, as is the Blessed Virgin herself. The intellect, however, has everything to fear, and not only the intellects of "the wise and intelligent ones," but the most holy, profound and indispensable Christian intellect, able to nourish a heart with truth, itself having "no stone on which to lay its head," since such a stone could only be the light of the Word. Faith's darkness and metaphysical darkness are the only true home of the intelligence here below, and the only security it can offer us. It is natural enough that the intellect should try to get away, but it is then that the situation becomes really frightening, especially for the heart which risks being thrown into worse aberrations. Faith is wrecked —and this is typical of the 20th century; intellect risks asphyxiating love, especially when it seeks less to support love than to work on its own account and to understand at any cost.[2]

The intellect then becomes fascinated by a single aspect of truth that it had been trying desperately to grasp, fatally neglecting, if it does not contradict, the other aspects by which this truth defies all efforts at possession. It ceases, as someone has said, "to hold onto both ends of the rope." This narrow approach is catastrophic to the heart, which needs vast scope—the full spectrum in which to breath—just as we ourselves required all the aspects of everyday life that no philosopher has ever been able to reduce to a perfect unity.[3]

In the case we are discussing, the *intellect* is not able to reduce all the aspects of the love of God to a single unity. It is even less able to reduce to a unity all the aspects of our condition as created beings facing our Creator, a situation the Jews had learned to live with long before the philosophers arrived or defined it. Theologians who are less pure than St. Thomas—and I dare to include St. Augustine—are in constant danger of trying to pass beyond our human limits instead of rendering them humble service. Insofar as the intellect very gradually nourishes love, it will point us toward God and toward that face-to-face vision. This voyage is a fearful undertaking for the intellect because as heaven comes closer, our spirit enters the "critical zone." For theologians as for everybody else (perhaps it is harder for theologians because they have fallen into the habit of always being right), there can be no apprenticeship of the Vision without a total shattering of our intellect. We must grow to accept the fact that one by one our poor little ideas are gently being splintered in the tender darkness of God.

Having said this, we can now dare to say something about the terrifying respect of God for our human liberty, a respect that even appears as helplessness in the case of Jacob's combat: "When he saw that he could not overcome Jacob. . . ." Here we enter the realm of the unthinkable. The All-Powerful may lay siege to man's spirit, infinitely desiring man's conversion, and yet this desire is not necessarily efficacious, as C. S. Lewis observed:

The problem is not simply that of a God who consigns some of his creatures to final ruin. That would be the problem if we were Mohammedans. Christianity, true, as always, to the complexity of the real, presents us with something knottier and more ambiguous—a God so full of mercy that he becomes man and dies by torture to avert that final ruin of his creatures, and who yet, where that heroic remedy fails, seems unwilling, or even unable, to arrest the ruin by an act of mere power. I said glibly a moment ago that I would pay "any price" to remove this *doctrine.* I lied. I could not pay one thousandth of the price that God has already paid to remove the *fact.* And here is the real problem: so much mercy, yet still there is hell.[5]

It is important that we do not massacre these truths by locking them into our clumsy intellects; rather, we should meditate on them, not in order to understand, but to learn to resist the temptation of wanting to understand at all costs, and constantly to keep dispelling the illusion of having understood.

God "Loves Less?"

Once more the root of the mystery is our own consistency before God, and we saw in Chapter 1 how hard it is to understand this. At the side of the infinite being of the Creator, there is a place for the limited being of the creature who remains distinct, yet adds nothing to the Creator. If we follow this truth through to the end, we shall stumble into the same difficulty as those who try to reconcile predestination and free will. Our liberty is, in fact, the most frightening consequence of our consistency. It is not just a twist in the all-powerfulness of God since it derives therefrom—and despite all, we really are incapable of contemplating at the same time his infinite power and our own freedom. In fact, by some instinct of self-preservation, our intellect resists too deep a contemplation of either end of this rope (excepting, of course, where one aspects of truth is squarely sacrificed to the other).

I would like to make an end to this kind of timid thinking. Whatever happens, intellect must suffer and die before entering into glory. By trying to spare it such a death, we run the risk of being left with nothing at all, neither the infinite power of God nor the disarming delicacy of his love. Both have to be contemplated totally, the first in adoration—acknowledging the total power of the Creator over our liberty, his irresistible power to save us when he wishes and to turn aside even our very rebellious wills.

Yet his gentleness and his delicacy also must be considered in their fullness. We can do this by trying to understand the disconcerting image he shows us of himself in the Bible. Here it is not just a question of justice and mercy; the reaction of God when faced with sin is far more disconcerting, and it can certainly not be reduced to mercy or more or less indifferent justice, an indifference that reminds us of the analysis made by certain theologians of whom we have spoken,[6] who maintain that God punishes some because he loves them less than he does others to whom he shows mercy, and that is that!

Already on purely theological grounds, such an idea is unacceptable since divine wisdom measures the *effects* of his love for us and not that love itself because the heart of God is infinite. God has only one kind of love and that is all he can give. God is unchanging, and one can scarcely suppose that *he has different feelings* toward some people than toward others. It is our own relation to his unique love that varies according to the attitude we freely adopt toward him.

When we open the Bible, the idea of a God who loves some less than others appears as a real betrayal of what he *seems* to feel in the face of sin—pain and anger. It is impossible to receive this revelation and to nourish our prayer with it if we persuade ourselves that God loves the sinner less than he loves the faithful servant. A rereading of the reproaches for Good Friday will certainly show that such an idea would be a death blow to revealed truth. If we believe that God can love less, we are incapable of seriously believing in his love for sinners. For the face of Christ, defenseless, sorrowful, "wounded to the bottom of his heart," with a love that remains infinite but respects our liberty, we substitute purely and simply a lesser love which abandons the sinner, leaving him to his own devices with a sort of non-predilection, that is to say, indifference.

Wounded to the Heart

Through the eyes of love, God's anger is very easy to understand, for it is a true and inevitable reaction to frustration, a reaction abundantly proclaimed in the Old Testament and confirmed in the New. Faced with this teaching, human sensibilities can be touched to the quick. The skepticism of unbelievers grows more smug and disdainful: a God who shows anger is no god, and the whole thing is an idealized projection of human psychology at its worst.

These reactions cannot be exorcised in a few words, and I admit to audacity when I present God's anger as a revelation of the deep secret of God, a secret by which we are swept into a region of excessive light where our ideas must be shattered. If the love of God for us has any meaning, his desire for our response has meaning too, and the wound we inflict by our refusal has been recognized as final and irrevocable, the anger that is the final touch confirming the truth, the gravity, the reality of such love. And so by refusing, we refuse to stay to the end where the Word really would have allowed us to enter into his light.

One readily accepts the idea that God is *offended* by sin, but theologians hate to endorse the many biblical and liturgical expressions suggesting that he is wounded, let alone caused to suffer, by sin. "God is impassive, etc., etc." and the machine that tramples over the most delicate truths is thrown into gear. And if we chance to ask the meaning of the current "You are hurting Jesus," the reply, more or less nuanced, is always, "It means absolutely nothing."

I feel obliged to repeat that all this is a bullet in the heart of Christianity, because it voids our belief of all meaning. To say that God is saddened by our sins does not mean that he suffers in the human sense of the word, but it does mean *something*, and the Holy Spirit makes use of these expressions because he can find no better words in which to convey his meaning. Jesus Christ daily invites the Church to remember his passion. Yet how are we to be expected to meditate in a perspective where sin offends the majesty of God without offending his love? And how could his love be offended without suffering a wound? Generally speaking, offending someone attacks his dignity, not his tenderness, unless his very tenderness be hurt by the "ingratitude and scorn" of those whom he loves.

The Bible does not so much talk of offense as of *irritation*. What is there in God that can be irritated by sin? Jealousy of his glory? How much simpler, then, not to have created so that the glory remains intact. The praise of the Three among themselves would then have remained infinitely perfect, and all creation, even Christ himself, would have appeared radically as useless servants of this glory. I say servants, because the creature cannot be fulfilled in any other perspective, and useless, because the service so rendered explains nothing of the existence of the creature of whom God has no need.

We have wondered at the secret decision in the heart of God to create, to give himself, to send his Son into this world; we have wondered at this mystery, not to reduce it to our stature but that we might lose ourselves within it by understanding that we understand nothing, and by realizing that it is not enough to consider the glory of God, for he is neither benefited nor increased by our praise. *God created us, he created the world about us, and to save us he became flesh—because he loves us.* The mystery is not dispelled by these words; on the contrary, it has become more impenetrable than ever. All we have accomplished is the removal of the arbitrary appearance that the mystery would have worn had we been content with the explanation that God's motives in creating are impenetrable. They are in harmony with the wisdom to which God himself wants to initiate us by revealing that he loves us. We are put to rout by such truth; it is far more upsetting than an absence of explanation. To those who feel the full weight of this love it is more incomprehensible than the evident uselessness of the creature.

More incomprehensible and yet the light is more brilliant! The Word of love closes no doors; rather we are invited to enter and to gaze into the unfathomable depths. The light of God is more crushing to our intellect than is the darkness when we stand outside the light, and yet it is light and thus nourishment. An intellect that is aware of the love of God and questions what that means is dragged into terrifying depths, more terrifying than anything that happens to an intellect that is unaware. The unknowing intelligence, even though it have a sense of God's glory, grapples with the void, whereas the one *who knows* comes to grips with reality. Reality lays hold of him and bears him away into unendurable splendor.

The Anger of Love

Seen in this light, God's anger is the most eloquent sign—more eloquent than his mercy—that he does not love us merely *for the fun of it*. God is in revolt against the mystery of evil with its eternal consequences, just as we are, and more than we are. We hesitate to understand this because of the trouble we have in ridding ourselves of the temptation (nourished by the stiffening of the Augustinian position) of attributing to God an infinitesimal share in the responsibility for hell's eternity. "He could, if he would. . . ." And going on from there, we find it hard to admit that he is totally innocent of everything, of absolutely everything, even of hell's eternity. He is as defenseless as the innocent child whose features he wears, as defenseless as that child when faced with implacable denial.

We might ask: How can God be "in revolt"? Surely there is no revolt in God. Surely there is only love. Have we not agreed that we cannot attribute sentiments[7] to him and that wisdom determines the effects of his love while respecting the freedom of just men and sinners?

Precisely: the *unrelenting* stubbornness of his infinite love assumes the face of wrath in the eyes of those who resist him. "Cursed by God," the Curé of Ars was wont to say, "by God who only knows how to bless!" Malediction then wears the features of benediction for him who refuses benediction.

God renounces the conversion of those who have chosen to lose themselves; this is true. But his abandon does not mean indifference, or, even less, love: he abandons in anger. And in the end this *non-indifference* will be resplendent with the glory of outraged love. Rage eternally manifests that *where God has abandoned conversion, he has not abandoned love*, for his love can never be removed. Love must protest eternally that it is not resigned to sin, and this protest, being the anger of love, is also its glory. This is the reason why, in spite of sin, love is permitted to remain eternally happy. No matter what we do, we shall never succeed in causing God and his elect to stop loving us, and so to stop being happy. Angela de Foligno discovered this when she found herself loving demons, and rejoicing because of them: O depth! depth!

If the damned could really cause God to become as indifferent as we claim him to be when we refuse the dogma of hell, they would succeed both in delivering themselves of their torments and in hurling God into the woe of no longer being God because he is no longer love. God is impassive and incapable of suffering because his love for us is too great. His love is infinite, and he is unable to stop being love, that is to say, the pure act that no suffering can touch. The whole mystery lies before us as we try to understand why this love concerns us. Our reflections have by no means dissipated it, but rather have rendered it more obscure in showing with what violence this love does concern us—even to taking on the features of human passions at their highest anguish, and continuing in the face of our ugly refusals, continuing to the very end of itself, into infinity.

And so we glimpse some of the depths of the words: "When he saw that he could not overcome Jacob. . . ." In spite of appearances and even if our heads are spinning, we must know for a fact that the love of God can never capitulate, and so this very obstinacy takes on the face of rage or of mercy according to the manner in which we receive it.

The Wound of the Hip

The love of God is timid? And yet, in our lives and in the world, there are upheavals that do not point to too much discretion on the part of God. His anger, when provoked by the very doubtful zeal of Job's friends, seemed to embody itself in shattering, atrocious events that made it so very obvious even to the least delicate of spirits. In fact, the events were real; they were permitted and even willed by God. The most authentic prophets and even Jesus Christ himself never hesitated to threaten the most terrifying catastrophe against all the disobedient peoples of Yahweh and *a fortiori* of the whole world (women of Jerusalem, Tower of Siloam, end of the world).

What about this timidity then? First, let us remember the permanent danger threatening us that is far graver than all the punishments that upset our nerves. We are in danger of refusing God for all eternity, and, I repeat, he is innocent of causing this risk. Furthermore, the risk we are running is more or less incomprehensible to us; we can scarcely imagine the danger we are in. Had God contented himself with showing us only his real face, so infinitely defenseless and tender, we should never have been able to understand anything at all. His delicate call would not only have seemed as insipid to us as the manna that made the Hebrews sick, but, much more simply, we would not have heard it at all. With our rough palates, we need have no worry about running away from the excessive refinement of God's

love—we do not even perceive it. "If God were proud,"
wrote C. S. Lewis, "he would hardly have had us on
such terms. But he is not proud; he stoops to conquer."[8]

No matter what the significance of the calamities
that batter the world or of the dire threats of prophecy
wherein we fancy that we see divine wrath,[9] one thing is
sure. These signs are forerunners, preparing the way for
the real visit of God in our hearts, just as the storm
sweeping the sky introduces a transparency that will
reflect the light with greater subtlety. We read in the
Book of Kings:

> Then Yahweh himself went by. There came a
> mighty wind so strong it tore the mountains and
> shattered the rocks before Yahweh. But Yahweh
> was not in the wind. And after the wind came an
> earthquake. But Yahweh was not in the earth-
> quake. After the earthquake came a fire. But Yah-
> weh was not in the fire. And after the fire came the
> sound of a gentle breeze. And when Elijah heard
> this, he covered his face with his cloak and came
> out and stood at the entrance to the cave (1 Kgs.
> 19:11-13).

This passage covers the various phases, becoming
more and more interior, of Christ's descent into us and
into the world. First, we are devastated on the surface
by a mighty wind; then we are stricken to the foundations by an earthquake. We are devoured internally by
fire that only ceases causing pain when we are suf-
ficiently purified and able to recognize his true face: the
murmuring of a gentle breeze, the illusive breath of the
Spirit, the constant murmur of an infinitely delicate

love at work within our being, at work beyond even the unknowable depths.

"*When he saw that he could not overcome Jacob, he touched the socket of Jacob's thigh. . . .*" This wounding of the socket of the hip exists at every stage of God's invasion, and each time it is more penetrating and more intimate. Describing these stages constitutes a superhuman task because of the infinite variety of nuances of the wound and because of its permanence, its depth and its simplicity. Nevertheless, we can try to trace the main lines.

The Mighty Wind and the Earthquake

The first strokes of battle serve to rough-hew the combatant, snatching away the most obvious obstacles separating him from God. Setting aside the great trials that stem from the mystery of the redemption,[10] we find that these obstacles center in the disappointments that wound man in his most cherished enthusiasms and his dearest hopes. Love and ambition, the two great passions of the human heart, as Pascal tells us, are consistent targets. Often, it is our noblest ambitions and our purest loves that God thwarts, seemingly at his pleasure.

At the age of twenty, our love, no matter how pure or ideal, always contains a dose of illusion as large as a mountain and a base of pride as hard as a rock. Youth, in its impulsive illusions, is more or less aware of the difficulties, but always profoundly certain of finding within self the resources required to surmount every obstacle. We can be considered young, in the sense of naive, as long as we have not yet learned to accept failure as a normal and very fundamental part of our lives. And we remain young a very long time; one experience can teach us to grow. The apostles, for example, paid dearly for their initiation, for the prize is always more costly where it meets the greatest resistance. Often, we find ourselves confronted by God precisely because of what seems to be the most beautiful things in our lives, even his service. We are like children with candy in our fist refusing to let go, and whose parents are obliged to slap their hands before they will open their fingers. So it is that God is obliged to cut us down to size; to do this, he sends that mighty wind. Simultaneously, the rock of our pride receives its first blow. One such blow is certainly not sufficient to reduce that pride to dust but the crack often allows the first salutary tears to flow. Of these, I shall say more later.

The earthquake is less spectacular but more enduring. Not only are the mountain of our illusions and the rock of our pride shaken, but also the very ground on which we stand. Our very equilibrium is threatened this time, as the foundations, and not merely the spire, of the building are attacked. Our deepest motives are challenged, as is our confidence in life, in others, even in God. We are torn from our staunchest supports, those on which we thought we might depend in all security. The effect of these shocks is not so much suffering as a gradual immersion into uneasiness, a state of insecurity, of helplessness that may even go so far as distress, something like that of a man who is thrown unprepared into interplanetary weightlessness.

"Do you know, Sir, what it is like no longer to know where to go?"[11] We get into a state like that in this earthquake, and it goes on for a long time. We don't know what to hang on to; we don't even know where we are. I must repeat that in this kind of thing, the more effective situations are not the most violent but the longest lasting, the most insidious, the situations that wear us down, and might, if prolonged indefinitely, plunge us into a Kafka-like situation, that is, into neurosis. God sometimes permits this to come about, but more often he does not, as long as we are flexible enough to abandon the supports we have clung to in time. If we can accept this loss of footing, we allow ourselves to fall into a void which little by little opens beneath our feet, and at the bottom we fall into the arms of God.

It is hard to offer examples because this intimate "earthquake" is so closely related to individual psychology. A situation that could be a thorn in the heart of one person might barely bruise the heart of another, leaving him perfectly intact. Now we are coming closer to the new Name that each of us is to receive in eternity, and which is to be written on the white stone of the Apocalypse. Only God really knows our weak spot, this thigh socket that he must strike so that we may gradually become infirm. After all, it is a secret between God and each of us. That is why we often hide this wound so very well not only from others but even from ourselves, which is a far more serious matter. Being able to recognize the wound is the first decisive step.

The most generous spirits are the ones most in need of enlightenment because, as we have seen, the combat concerns them above all, and they run the risk of being the most upset by what is happening to them. They see an instrument of perdition in what is actually leading them to God—to wit, the loss of the very thing they had been counting on to get them there.

When I Could No Longer Move

Some of these young Christians have married in
order to find Christ through human love, and that love
has not kept its promises. They are frustrated, seemingly by the loss of the mainstay of their spiritual life, the
riches of Christian marriage that the Church had told
them about, or else their love has flourished so beau-
tifully that it has become an obstacle between their
souls and God. And yet here they are, condemned to
detach themselves spiritually just as much as those who
had renounced him from the start. Both groups are
going through the apprenticeship of which St. Paul
spoke: "It remains that those who have wives act as if
they had none" (1 Cor. 7:29). Such an apprenticeship
would be impossible without this prolonged earthquake,
stretching down through the years, working away in
that wound in the socket of the thigh, that is to say, the
nerve center of the spirit. For "all sickness is not unto
death but for the glory of God" (Jn. 11:4).

Meditation will never be sufficient to make these
truths a part of us. They will have to penetrate right to
our core. And no amount of clever thinking can ever
bring us to the point of "those who use this world as if
not using it" (1 Cor. 7:31) unless this grace be granted
to us from above. From below, it will come from the
very infirmity of our flesh when time has done its work
on us.

Turning to those men and women who have left all
to consecrate themselves to God's service, we find that
the same hard truths are operative. Yet the very way of
life they have chosen makes these truths all the more
indispensable and yet harder to accept. This time the
values at stake are the most precious of all, supernatu-

ral values destined to crumble away little by little before our eyes as the result of the earthquake. And among these values are the very ones on which we had hoped to build.

Now, as the precious pearl itself seems to disintegrate, we are reminded of the biblical passages about the sacrifice of Abraham. Losing a son is always cruel —and still more cruel if he is meant to be sacrificed at his father's hands. And yet Abraham's anguish went even deeper, for his son had been given to him by God as the pledge of innumerable posterity. God contradicted himself, and this is why Abraham's trial was, above all, a test of faith. The test we are meditating on here is just such a test. It is a pity that so often this trial is reduced to a simple exhortation to keep faith in the teeth of disappointments. Abraham's reaction sprang from quite a different source, one that was infinitely deeper than a mere "holding on." One must know how to love in order to attain Abraham's kind of purity, to "hope against hope," to love so greatly that hope and faith—no longer the result of will power, even heroic will power—become in all truth the very fruits of helplessness, the despairing helplessness of inextinguishable love.

Feeling the presence of God in certain realities, we have sacrificed all; we have sold our goods to buy that pearl of precious price. And then little by little these realities crumble. The missionary on his way to become a fisher of men finds himself shut up in a petty administration job for years and years. No matter what may happen, all apostles, all priests, are condemned to rot in one place (Jn. 12:24) one day or another. Being "reliable" is not enough to keep a man faithful to his post, because the soul of a priest is invaded by a desert that is

not ordinary desert. It is the desert of Mount Horeb
and of the encounter with God. And unless some obscure knowledge of this encounter steadies his faith, as if
drawing him through an air vent, "the rain will fall and
the floods come and the winds blow and the ruin of that
house will be very great indeed" (Mt. 7:27).

The disappointments that beset contemplatives are
even more subtle and baffling, because they have a
bearing on realities that are the more intimate, being
attached somehow to God himself—for example, the
liturgy in the case of Benedictines, penance for Trap-
pists, prayer for Carmelites, theology for Dominicans,
poverty for Franciscans, etc. Each finds God ever more
deeply according to the road that is his own. It is the
story of the white stone over and over again! The earthquake destroys the road that the contemplatives have
come to consider as their own, making it dangerous or
downright impractical, a process similar to the one we
pointed out as regards human love. Liturgy, asceticism,
theology and prayer do not fulfill their bright promises,
or else they fulfill them too rigidly. Even here, as we
see, we must use all things as if not using them.

This is why these trials scoop out such a deep
wound. They are nothing similar to what we had been
expecting and for which we had been reserving our very
special generosity. They undermine us, finding their
way into the deep recesses of our being, sapping our
strength. Our resistance turns to panic as we find ourselves more and more incapable of turning to God for
whom we have left everything. Yet when we are no
longer able to go to him by our own rough and clumsy
initiatives, he comes, in all his purity, to us: "For when
I am weak, then I am strong" (2 Cor. 12:10). In other
words, when I can no longer move, when I have become

relaxed and flexible, God is at last able to come to me at his ease, to take hold of me and invest me with his strength.

The only trouble is that we do not understand this; we cannot understand it and so we fight and struggle in this combat of love that is so stupid and so sacred, just as Jacob did in his combat with the angel.

The Inevitable Betrayal

This combat reaches its point of culmination in the Gospels where Christ struggled with his apostles, a struggle that began in their very first encounter. Every word, every gesture of the Master hammered away at the apostles, splintering and overturning their firmest convictions. "Do you not understand? Men of little faith, why have you doubted? If your faith were as big as a grain of mustard seed . . . . Why do you call me good, you who are bad?"

The apostles could not get used to Christ's miracles either; they were always stupefied at the start, a kind of marveling stupefaction that was often mixed with fright. For each attempt to walk upon the water in the wake of such a man ended in sinking like a stone, in a scurrying back to solid ground, ground that grew less and less solid, however, as a result of the continuing contact with a power that made everything totter in and around the apostles.

Within their hearts and minds, above all, the doctrine of Christ unleashed a series of seismic quakes that literally drove them to cry out, "This is a hard saying; who can listen to it?" And Jesus, knowing in himself that his disciples were murmuring, said to them:

" 'Does this scandalize you? What then if you should see the Son of Man ascending to where he was before?' . . . From this time on, many of his disciples turned back and no longer went about with him" (Jn. 6:61-63, 67).

"Blessed is he who is not scandalized in me" (Mt. 11:6), that is to say, who does not come to grief. Even the twelve narrowly avoided this scandal; "Jesus therefore said to the twelve, 'Do you also wish to go away?' and Simon Peter answered, 'Lord, to whom shall we go? You have the words of eternal life, and we have come to believe and to know that you are the Christ, the Son of God' " (Jn. 6:68-70).

One can imagine that such traumatic experiences seared the hearts of these men with burning fissures, ever deepened by the words of Christ, "For the word of God is living and efficient and keener than a two-edged sword" (Heb. 4:12). " 'And I say to you that whoever puts away his wife and marries another commits adultery.' His disciples said to him, 'If the case of a man with his wife is so, it is not good to marry.' He said to them, 'Not all can accept this teaching, but only those to whom it has been given' " (Mt. 19:9-10).

The language become still tougher when Jesus speaks of wealth after the defection of the rich young man: " 'With great difficulty will they who have riches enter the Kingdom of heaven. . . . It is easier for a camel to pass through the eye of a needle than for the rich man to enter into the Kingdom of God.' But they were astonished the more, saying among themselves, 'Who then can be saved?' Jesus looked at them and said, 'With man it is impossible, but not with God, for all things are possible with God' " (Mk. 10:23-27).

The perpetual tension comes to the breaking point

with the announcement of the mystery of the cross: " 'Store up these words in your mind: the Son of Man is to be betrayed into the hands of men.' But they did not understand this saying. It was hidden from them that they might not perceive it, and they were afraid to question him" (Lk. 9:44-45).

When he insisted, forcing them to understand, their revulsion turned to outright revolt: "From that time on, Jesus began to show his disciples that he must go to Jerusalem and suffer many things from the elders and the scribes and the chief priests, be put to death, and on the third day rise again. And Peter, taking him aside, began to chide him, saying: 'Far be it, Lord, that such a thing should happen to you.' He turned and said to Peter, 'Get behind me, Satan; you are a scandal to me; for you are not minding the things of God but those of men' " (Mt. 16:21-23).

To the very end Peter was obsessed by the desire to "avoid all that" by means of his own personal courage, an obsession shared by the disciples who wanted to turn all their love to the defense of the Master's life. "Thomas who is called the Twin, said to his fellow disciples, 'Let us also go [to Jerusalem] that we may die with him!' " (Jn. 11:16). To the last they tried to resist by every means at their disposal, even to slicing the ear of the high priest's servant, to avoid the arrest of the one they loved. Only when Jesus objected to their intervention that "the Scriptures might be fulfilled," only then did all the disciples leave him and flee (Mt. 26:56), feeling somehow that they had been abandoned rather than having abandoned him, that they had been abandoned in the efforts they had been ready to make to save him at the risk of their own lives.

"Behold, Satan has desired to have you that he

may sift you like wheat" (Lk. 22:31). The shock this time was too great; it derived not from the events but from the conduct of Jesus himself. "Had I been there with my Franks," Clovis cried, "everything would have been different." And according to Péguy, Joan of Arc revolted with all her being against "those who allowed such things to happen." Yet neither saw that the real problem was Jesus himself when he made the humanly unacceptable decision to be "to the Jews indeed a stumbling block and to the Gentiles foolishness" (1 Cor. 1:23). "No one takes my life from me but I lay it down myself" (Jn. 10:18). With all the good will in the world and in spite of their love and their heroism, the apostles *were not able*[12] to follow Jesus Christ over such terrain. To understand this, we must remember Peter and what it was that Peter lacked, for we, too, are in danger of lacking in the same way, a lack that makes us, as it made Peter, unable to follow Christ to the very end. It is not a lack of faith—"I have prayed for you that your faith may not fail" (Lk. 22:23)—and it was not a lack of love—" Peter said to him . . . 'I will lay down my life for you' " (Jn. 11:16). It is easy enough to find fault with the apostles' failure to understand and with their presumption, but it is not so easy to "count the cost" of the effort we must make not to fall victim to the same presumption.

What they lacked was a certain attitude, without which it is impossible to tune in to the divine power, just as a radio that is not properly set cannot pick up certain broadcasts. It is absolutely impossible for us to adopt this attitude or to start off in the right direction unless God himself has set us on the course to the combat that we have been considering—the combat of Jacob. During its course no vicissitudes will be spared to any but the very pure. The story of the apostles is the typical story of men of good will.

Of course, Peter might have been better off had he been able to let himself be crushed, for this would have saved him a betrayal. But he did not dream that such a thing could happen to him; he would never have admitted the possibility of being crushed. And thus he was obliged as the first Pope to proclaim in person and to the end of time the infallible fruit of a certain concept of Christian life. At the point at which they were before the passion, Peter and the apostles could not have acted any differently,[13] and neither could anyone else without suffering the same rout, the same overwhelming prostration, the same interior disaster that was to strike them down. Not so much by his death, but by his refusal to defend himself or to show his power, Christ in truth drained all strength from the apostles. They were no longer able to follow him, and there was actually a moment of darkness and revolt when they did not even want to follow him. All this was inevitable until the moment when Peter's eyes were opened and he was able once more to strengthen his brothers.

The Beginnings of a Strange Flavor

What was it that caused Peter's eyes to open? Here we come to the critical point, where the wound has penetrated deeply into the socket of the thigh, the point where Jacob's hip joint was loosened during his combat with God—the point where the earthquake, its work done, gives place to something entirely different. "And the Lord turned and looked at Peter, and Peter remembered the Lord's words. He had said 'Before the cock crows you will deny me three times.' And Peter went out and wept bitterly" (Lk. 22:61-62).

The wound had pierced through to his most intimate being, to which from the very start the Holy Spirit had been laying siege. The beatitude of tears is not to be found on the nervous level, and neither is it caused by a heart that is too tender. The beatitude of tears springs, in fact, from our hearts of stone at the very moment when God has found the breach that he has perhaps sought for years, and finding it at last refreshes it with his tenderness.

And so Peter, flooded by pain and joy, was transfixed by the *coup de grace* which forevermore made an end to his resistance. Despite his bitterness, he felt no shame in that instant but rather a great sense of deliverance. Even as, with consternation, he was tasting the ultimate and terrible fruit of his presumption and hardness of heart, he felt that the deepest, most cruel point of that hardness was leaving him forever; it was dissolving before an inrush of tenderness, hitherto unknown, that was pouring from the eyes of Jesus Christ. Peter understood that Jesus was not judging him, and that more than ever he was offering his life, as though he were somehow comforted, having at last found footing in Peter's heart even at the cost of betrayal. He understood that judgment is nothing other than the look of God at each of us in reply to our faults and beyond our faults—a look that leaves us to judge ourselves, each according to the manner in which he has received that unforeseeable love. "Everyone who falls upon that stone will be broken to pieces, but upon whomever it falls, it will grind him to powder" (Lk. 20:18; Mt. 21:44). Those who allow themselves to be broken to pieces will be delivered, but those who refuse will be crushed by the immense pressure of love.

Peter was no longer the same man when he re-joined his brothers. He came from another world, a world he had scarcely glimpsed but the certainty of whose reality was to carry him through grim relapses into doubt and distress during the course of the passion, a certainty that would begin to grow after the resurrection, resounding in his heart until the final great burst of Pentecost. Peter now looked upon his brothers in a new manner, surprising even himself. Watching their anxiety and despair throughout those dark hours, his look was new. It contained a strange new flavor; it was a look of pity.

You Have Not Yet Asked for Everything

Once the tears have been shed, the earthquake gives place to the "devouring fire" of Pentecost. Huge barriers have fallen. And although God was not present in the fire, the relationship between God and man was entirely changed. The combat has entered a new phase that might be thus defined: because Jacob was vanquished, Jacob was the winner. God had resisted him with all his might, yet once Jacob had been injured, God resisted no longer. From then on Jacob was able to get everything he wanted. In fact he seemed to be the master and God seemed to be the one who implored: "Then he said, 'Let me go; it is dawn.' But Jacob answered: 'I will not let you go until you bless me.' "

The Psalms say that God resists the proud, but that is an illusion which can be blamed upon the pride of the proud. God sets up no barriers on his side; the barriers are in the hearts of men. God resists our resistance by refusing to accept those barriers, by trying to overthrow them. This is true at the start of Jacob's combat; yet once the breach has been made, God no

longer tries to overcome our hardness by force but
rather by offering us the contact of his gentleness, gentleness that is utterly without defenses. Because, however, we are not yet gentle, because we are still impervi-
ous, that gentleness feels to us like a devouring fire,
more deeply cruel than the earthquake and yet somehow so infinitely sweet. God is not in the fire because
he is not cruel, and the painful, devouring impression of
his gentleness is an illusion stemming from our own
cruelty that still hangs on as our soul agonizes slowly,
liquefying in the heat of God. "The mountains melt like
wax before the Lord, before the Lord of all the earth"
(Ps. 96:5). The mountains of our hardness melt like
wax before the face of God.

The phase that we will now begin to consider is
that where prayer manifests easily its total power, God
is literally unable to resist real prayer. "If you have
faith like a mustard seed, you will say to this mulberry
tree, 'Be uprooted and be planted in the sea,' and it will
obey you" (Lk. 17:6; Mt. 17:20). "And I say, ask and it
shall be given to you, seek and you shall find, knock
and it shall be opened to you. For everyone who asks
receives, and he who seeks finds, and to him who
knocks it shall be opened" (Lk. 11:9-10). "Amen I say
to you, whoever says to this mountain, 'Arise and hurl
yourself into the sea,' and does not waver in his heart
but believes that whatever he says will be done, it shall
be done for him. Therefore, I say to you, all things
whatsoever you ask for in prayer, believe that you shall
receive and they shall come to you" (Mk. 11:23-24).
And lastly: "Heretofore you have not asked for anything in my name. Ask, and you shall receive that your
joy may be full" (Jn. 16:24).

Theologians teach that prayer is infallible when
salvation is perseveringly requested.[15] We can under-

stand, then, God's resistance to prayers demanding temporal and even spiritual goods that have no place in his plan for our salvation. But we must admit that he can also resist our prayers for essentials and keep us waiting for the most precious gifts, gifts that he intends to give us in the end. Evidently, then, we are under an obligation to pray perseveringly; I suppose it could be considered quite normal to hang around waiting for years and even for a lifetime. It is easy enough to say that this is "normal," but no one really accepts the idea without a certain rancor, or, at minimum, accepts it with a touch of sadness. Does God really hear us up there? He probably has other fish to fry, as we can see from the parable of the iniquitous judge and the importunate widow.

We get into the habit of thinking that God does not give in willingly and that he keeps mankind at arms' length. Fine! Let us then declare our submission and remain aloof with the idea that we are doing enough by resigning ourselves, since he can't very well expect us to be happy about it. Here begins the secret of Jansenism which was first of all a sadness before it became a doctrine—disillusionment at feeling God to be so distant and yet quite a comfort at not having to love him more, or to leave our shells, or to try to overcome obstacles that we are subconsciously pleased to blame on him. We become much attached to this false humility by which we strip God of his transcendence, and we accuse someone like St. Thérèse of pride—scoffing at her audacious confidence in expecting the grace that would make a saint of her, not tomorrow but here and now.

The Walls of Jericho

A grandmother I knew spent her life moving

among her numerous children to help them settle their problems. As her interference was not always entirely welcome, I suggested one day that the time was at hand for her to take a rest and to help her family by prayer and the search for God: "Well done, good and faithful servant; you have been faithful over a few things so I shall set you over many; enter into the joy of your Lord." I had hoped she would understand these words; instead, she replied, "When I was twenty I thirsted for God, and I wanted to set out to conquer him. Very soon I came up against a fortress that seemed impregnable. I said to myself: I will go all the way around and I shall find a breach. Starving, I circled around for months,[16] but I never did find one. I understood at last that I had been guilty of pride, that God was not for me and that I must give him up. Since that time I live—I drag myself through life—doing my duty and occupying myself with the dishes and the little daily worries."

This description would have been accurate had it been exactly the opposite. The citadel is our heart, and it is God who circles around trying to find a breach. When he does find one, it is that wound in the thigh. Indeed, this situation can go on for years, even for a whole lifetime, always giving the impression that God is resisting us and that he leaves us waiting at the door. In a sense, resignation to waiting is a good thing but not too much of it, or, rather, not that kind of resignation. It is not simply to amuse himself that God waits to open the door. His desire to give himself is infinitely greater than ours, and that is really the heart of the trouble. God wants us to persevere in prayer not for the sake of collecting indulgences but so that he may bring us to a certain *quality* of prayer, may provoke a certain tone to our sighing. Were we able to produce these right away, he would answer us at once. Perfect prayer is not only infallibly effective, it is *immediately* effective. God is unable to delay even for an instant his answer to such prayer. In fact, it is blasphemous to suppose that prayer coming from the Holy Spirit should be kept waiting even for an instant.[17] We are pretty quick to accuse God of resisting us. We put this down to his transcendence, injecting the ounce of pride that would be ours were we in his place. That is why I call this supposition blasphemous; among other things it justifies the loveless resignation that we offer him.

If there were in God the slightest speck of the self-complacency we attribute to him—and which perhaps accounts for the zeal of certain persons in claiming that God's gifts are entirely gratuitous—we should be justified in offering him the kind of resignation that begot sad-faced Jansenism. We had much better to listen to God himself speaking about his transcendence, for it is the transcendence of love. The only real homage our intellects can pay him is to refrain from premature conclusions and to think about him in fear and trembling—not fear of a caricature of majesty suited to our boorishness but rather fear that that very boorishness may spoil the infinitely gentle, illusive delicacy that love can honor in all purity.

After all, Job was praised in spite of his roars of despair. The pathetic violence of his seemingly disrespectful call for help honored God's transcendence far more than the edifying speeches of his friends for the simple reason that his violence was the violence of love. Job, in crazy, unconquerable hope—hope he had probably not even admitted to himself—expected some response from God, something his friends "would not allow themselves" to expect. Because transcendence *is* love, Job's expectation is justified: we are expected to expect all the miracles of salvation, all the happiness in "good measure, pressed down, shaken together, running over" pouring into our lap (Lk. 6:38).

If we are prepared to allow God to speak to us of his transcendence, we then understand his infinite impatience to give us *all things* as quickly as possible, so as to bring us to total happiness without delay. We shall begin to suspect that he is not to blame for the delay we suffer, in the same way that he cannot be blamed for hell. When there is no answer to our most praiseworthy prayers, we may be sure that it is not God's fault but our own. Perhaps because our hope is so feeble, we resign ourselves to delay too easily, and we insult God by imagining that he does not love us, at least with that extraordinary love whose transcendence we fail to recognize. Our lack of desire, our want of intelligence, even perhaps our laziness—all these we are pleased to call "patience," because we object to being upset by too violent a love, too swift a response. Alternately—and sometimes concurrently—we are horribly impatient, demanding instant response, not because we are hard pressed by charity but because we want to make an end to this painful state of desire, to the torments that love of God imposes. The fault is all on our side. Whether we are patient or impatient, it amounts to the same thing. We are trying to protect ourselves from the fire that Jesus came to cast upon the earth.

Our most fervent prayers oscillate between laziness and revolt, between hot and cold, without finding the right tone, the infintely soft and powerful note that brought down the walls of Jericho with a single blast. God waits in infinite desire to hear this note from us. He cares for us with a maternal tenderness—the visible expression of which he has placed in the hands of the Blessed Virgin that little by little, through the clumsy repetition of our stumbling prayers, we might learn the incredible whisperings of the Holy Spirit.

From Major to Minor

Nothing more than constant repetition is required for this sighing, this whispering to hollow out our hearts of stone, just as the steady dripping of water wears a hollow in the hardest rock. By dint of repeating the Our Father, the Hail Mary, the De Profundis, we may hope one day to recite an Our Father or Hail Mary that will gush *de profundis* from the very depths of our being, vibrating in perfect harmony with the desire of God. In that instant there will be fusion without any dissonance between prayer, forevermore undefended, and love that is infinitely defenseless.

> No, I would not your beauty choose
> Not in you myself could lose
> But in that certain something
> That I came upon by chance . . .

Thus sings St. John of the Cross. Yet God, too, searches our souls for that certain something that he hopes to chance upon. I refer to the whispering that alone can touch his heart because in reality it comes from his own heart. Until God has heard that note, until he has been able to extract it, he cannot let himself be touched; he cannot allow himself to be overcome. God offers no resistance; quite the contrary, for it is on account of his utterly helpless gentleness that he is *unable* to harmonize with anything but a gentleness as fluid as his own. Apart from this fluidity, there is no current that runs between God and man. And so man grows weary, and by dint of growing weary—as long as he does not give way to discouragement and perseveres in prayer—little by little his prayers will lose altitude, that is, they will shed the arrogance common to us all at the start. Keeling over like a wounded bird, he will drop slowly toward the wound of Jacob; reaching its center, vanquished, he will receive "far more than he could ask or conceive" (Eph. 3:30).

> Because so low, so low I stooped,
> So high, so very high I soared,
> That at last, at last I touched
> That which I had sought.[19]

The quality of the note is created by the infirmity, the exhaustion, the breaking of a voice when all pretension is dropped. A friend of mine, the father of a family, had a child who was unable to walk and who constantly asked his father to pick him up. The father, who would come home tired and rushed from work and feeling that, after all, it was a mother's job to pick up a child, admitted that his first impulse was always to refuse: "Oh, leave me alone!" The child would not answer, but soon he would begin again, this time in a softer voice, a lower tone, more gently: "Papa, pick me up." The third time around, the father would give in. The remarkable thing is that the child's tone grew softer instead of louder, and the last request was just a murmur. Remarkable, too, that it took three calls, as much to touch the father as for the son to find the golden tone the father was unable to resist. By no effort or contrivance could the first request feel out the inimitable whisper of a prayer grown faint with waiting. This transition from a major key to a minor is an immense event that takes place much as fruit ripens, when the heart has long been steeped; it is the slow wearing down of harshness that takes place during Jacob's combat.

The Wound That Reconciles Forever

This combat is no less than the interplay of the two purifications, active and passive, of which St. John of the Cross speaks. Active purification means perserverance in the effort of detachment, allowing charity to grow and breathe within us—perservering in prayer, tirelessly repeating formulas which seem to many people to be idiotic. And so they are, deplorably so, when prayer is repeated only for the sake of "sticking to the rules" and expecting nothing in return. And yet how magnificent it is to be idiotic, when one is worn out with gazing at the horizon, waiting for him who must come. Seen in this perspective, one is no longer the same person after ten rosaries; one is a little more exhausted, a little poorer, a little nearer to the final defeat.

Passive purification is the series of quakes and shocks during the course of which, thanks to prayer, God is at work on the hip wound. Dialogue is created between our assault on God by prayer and God's material assault on us through events and, at great depth, by the pressure of his love. To all appearances, there is a clash here between two forces; yet in secret they are accomplices, each hoping for the victory of the other. Our prayer does violence to the Kingdom, but it only encounters resistance when it lacks purity. In trying to overcome this resistance, prayer exhausts itself, and in losing strength grows more gentle until it is able to harmonize with the gentleness of God. Then all combat ceases: each has won because both have been vanquished though in a different manner. God has vanquished in advance because he wanted to give everything, though he ran into the obstacle of our pride which was searching for another kind of victory and so was unable to receive the one he offered without combat. God then fights that he may be vanquished. And we combat stupidly that we may lose the benefits of our victory. Furthermore, by defeating us at this crazy level on which we are fighting, he permits us to enter into possession of the crown he had offered us from the very beginning. Sin consists in being victorious on a level where victory is madness. The splendor and the misery of Jacob's combat was that despite himself he was fighting the battle of sin, even as he groaned inutterably for the defeat of his pride and the victory of his love. It is true enough to say that in this combat each side desires to be vanquished because both desire to love. The only obstacle is the pride that God must overthrow in order to be vanquished by our weakness, as we send forth that very pride to do battle with the secret desire of seeing it dissolved and dead. And so it was that God and Jacob welcomed the wound with the same joy, for they were reconciled for all time in the new gentleness that allowed Jacob to obtain everything that he wanted.

A Soft, Gentle Murmur

During the passion, Peter received the lance wound

of Jesus' gaze so that he might draw near to that gentleness, to that source of power. Between his trumpeting in the major key of "I shall give my life for you" and his murmur in the minor key of "Lord, you know all things; you know that I love you," there had to be betrayal and the bitter tears that sprang from it. No doubt, Peter might have been spared his treachery, but something big was required in any case in order to obtain the tears and the resulting transition from major to minor in his prayers.

From that day ownward, Peter possessed in the depths of his heart the perfect weapon giving him power over the heart of God—his infirmity and his constant awareness of it: "The sun rose on him just as he left Phanuel, limping because of his thigh."

To be sure, Peter did not realize it at first, and it took him quite a while to get used to the game of "the loser wins." And yet he held its secret: "For when I am weak, then I am strong" (2 Cor. 12:10). Little by little he got the feel of this new game, the game of love, and it became for him a source of living water, springing forth toward eternal life; at the same time it was a devouring fire, the fire that Jesus had come "to cast upon the earth, and what will I but that it be kindled" (Lk. 12:49).

"I will not let you go until you bless me." These very words became a flame in the heart of Jacob, nourished by his consciousness of God's gentleness toward him. "Let me go; it is dawn" were the first words spoken by Yahweh during the combat. They allowed a little of his defenseless tenderness to show and his desire to be overcome, to "gird himself and serve" (Lk. 12:37), and this with an undreamed-of and most distressing humility that will be his eternal attitude. At that moment the dawn of eternal life broke before the eyes of Jacob and he began to understand that he had won.

The combat, however, was not yet over; the rough presence of a hostile God must give place to the subtle, elusive God of love. And since Jacob was not quite at the right level yet, the combat had to go on—though in a quite different tone, the indescribable tone of two breaths in search of each other. Once he had learned to wait, Jacob saw that in fact God was not really resisting him, but that God was unable to surrender totally as long as his own gift was not pure and defenseless.

Then it was God who begged, who begged Jacob to understand: it is not my fault but the hour has not yet come. We are not at the same stage, you and I, and yet you are beginning to understand, and the dawn is here, and let me leve so that I may return to you in completeness, more secretly and with exceeding joy. It is expedient for you that I depart, because if I do not go, the Paraclete will not come to you, but if I go I will send him to you (cf. Jn. 16:7).

Jesus, too, in a sort of supplication was to say to Mary Magdalene: "Do not touch me for I have not yet ascended to my Father" (Jn. 20:17). The theme was the same: everything was new and yet all was not yet over. But the hearts of men had grown permeable, and it was no longer an epiphany that lay ahead but rather an invisible descent into the most intimate depths of the soul, during which God would give himself totally in the darkness as he would do later in the light. In the burning darkness of Pentecost, the combat had become an anguish of inexpressible gentleness and inexpressible pain.

Then it was that Elias began to hear the soft, gentle murmur, the whistling of a gentle air, and he covered his face with his cloak. After the squalls and showers of spring, the storms and the heat of summer, the inward turning of autumn, comes the repose and silence of winter. The world is covered with snow. Christian life assumes its true nature: a long night watch, gentle and monotonous, a time of patient consuming waiting for the One who is to come. Those who have understood allow themselves to fade away, to dissolve into foggy insipid grayness. "For you have died and your life is hidden with Christ in God. When Christ, your life, shall appear, then you too will appear with him in glory" (Col. 3:3-4).

On that day, at last, we shall speak.

NOTES

1. Perhaps it was to help us understand this that he first presented himself as a child in the mystery of Christmas before he manifested it in his death and resurrection.

2. I dare say that even the theology of St. Thomas (insofar as the great doctor's humility piously welcomes the Augustinian tradition, which, despite everything, is a humane one) can sometimes be dangerous for souls in this domain where the most infinitesimal impurity encourages the devil to ravage, or at least to oppress the hope of, the "little ones" to whom God the Father spoke through Christ ("Father, I praise you . . ."). This is why St. Francis de Sales renounced Augustinianism in favor of a less solid, less structured theology, which, however, preserved an unlimited confidence, confidence to which we are invited by St. Thérèse of Lisieux in the wake of Jesus himself. This invitation is the marrow of the Church's message, encouraging as it does all the timid hearts for whom St. Thérèse wrote.

Looking back at the Carmelite quoted earlier, I would

say that, no doubt, her initiation to St. Thomas was necessary and right, but I think that she might also have been introduced to *something else* at the same time—something that at first glance seems incompatible with St. Thomas, but which better accords with grace and human liberty as the infinity of God accords with the nature of created man.

But what if we do not see this? I think St. Francis de Sales' solution is the best, since above all we must keep our confidence and our spontaneity, whereas the nun was afraid of having lost these. In her case I cannot help seeing pure evil as regards this loss, a dry loss such as the pastoral Church wishes to avoid at any cost. If it were absolutely necessary to sacrifice Thomism to preserve the sale of confidence, I would not hesitate for a moment to sacrifice it. However, if all Thomists were to agree with me, perhaps such a sacrifice would not be required, and all Christians would benefit by the crucifying light, without diminishing in the slightest the intensity of their confidence but causing it to pass through a purifying fire, refining the ideas on which such confidence rests but which are always too rough-grained.

3. The light of the Word is needed here. The only healthy philosophy is one that refuses systems of thought and renounces rationalistic unification that is really deadly. The Scholastics would call such a system univocal.

4. And, at that, they would not achieve the intellectual balance of St. Thomas, which rested on radical acceptance of imperfection.

5. C. S. Lewis, *The Problem of Pain*, pp. 107-108.

6. See Chapter 1, note 8.

7. Lewis, pp. 107-108.

8. *Ibid.*, p. 85.

9. Adoration teaches us to pass beyond this problem without resolving it (cf. Chapter One).

10. It is hard to say how God makes use of all the traumatisms that so crush the human heart, since their very violence seems to make their victims incapable of offering them up, having lost all sense of human consistency.

11. Marmeladoff to Raskolnikov in Dostoevski's *Crime and Punishment*.

12. This is not to say they were innocent. We should not forget St. Jerome and "those unable to love" who were condemned by their very helplessness. Without going as far as

that, the disciples' inability to follow Jesus stemmed from the extraordinary impurity found even in the most generous hearts, impurity that has been described by St. John of the Cross in great detail.

We can no more avoid this impurity than we can avoid original sin, and yet we are condemned by it. Our helplessness, which is at once a sin and a misfortune, calls forth mercy. Had there been merely a question of misfortune, there would have been no need of forgiveness. Had it been only a sin, there would have been no remedy. But since it is both, it has irreplaceable power over the mercy of God: this is the whole story of the lost sheep.

13. Cf. note. 12 above.

14. "Everyone who drinks of this water will thirst again. He, however, who drinks of the water that I will give him shall never thirst" (Jn. 4:13-14).

15. There is another condition, and we shall speak about it: "devotion" or, if you prefer, "piety." It is the inimitable tone of prayer in poverty.

16. "They snarl like dogs and prowl about the city; they wander about like scavengers" (Ps. 58:15-16).

17. "Father, I give you thanks that you have heard me. Yet I know that you always hear me" (Jn. 11:41-42).

18. The mixture of very lofty truths and a homeopathic dose of pride is terribly explosive, and it can cause fearful ravage in the domain of hope. Nothing is more dangerous than to imagine one's own version of divine transcendence— precisely because it is transcendent—and to make oneself the champion of its rights. Here again is the temptation of Job's friends, which consisted in taking God's side *against men*. Of course, great jealousy for God's glory could be the cause at the outset, but I must insist that there is nothing more dangerous as long as even the most infinitesimal speck of pride trails around in our souls. This pride fastens onto transcendence, defending its privileges while secretly appropriating them and lifting itself to their level by according itself the glory of claiming them and pouring into these claims all the bitter jealousy common to pride defending its own. The only remedy to all this is Job's attitude; we cannot meditate on this enough.

19. St. John of the Cross, *Poems*.